Ch 9: A guy yuk
new be devai

Ch 10: eyes off your phone, crowds,
tables @ restaurants, lines, waiting room,
gas pump, groceny, smile, say hi, ask a?

Ch 11: Go to family and friend functions w/ an open
mind - and alone - weddings, showers, reunions
even funerals

Where Are the Good Guys?

The Single Woman's Guide
to Meeting Mr. Right *Offline*

Ch 12: Go to any local parties w/ an eye for meetup
or host one.

Ch 13: Start a meetup group or find one.
Men frequent technology, business, BJ groups
D R Baby Steppers Group.

Ch 14: If you are really shy, sit back,
make eye contact, smile warmly, and
let him lead. Have a few questions
prepared in case he is shy, too.

Judith Joshel

Ch 15: ~~Chamber of Commerce~~, Toastmasters, or
Business Conventions

Ch 16: Men who like sports are plentiful, so it
is worth developing an interest or at
least ask who they think is going
to win.

Ch 7: Google "hiking clubs" or Sierra Club

Ch 18 People need to eat - be friendly, sit in communal area, ask re: menu.

Ch 19   Auto shop or dept - ask a car related question

Ch 20   Home depot "how to workshops - also learn a new skill

Ch 21 -   autoparts - ask re: your model car

Ch 22 .   nurseries ask b/how to grow a certain plant

Ch 23   Follow your bliss so you meet a likeminded person. Dances often have lessons! Choir? ✓ Meet up

Ch 24   Chorus, writing, film meet up groups

Ch 25   Consider denominational groups - meet ups, classes, conventions colleges

Ch 26   Spiritual Retreat Centers such as GlennEyrie Men often connect in nature & physical activities

Ch 27 Maybe a dog would help me relax a little - at least to volunteer or walk dog park.

Gifts for My Readers

I invite you to enjoy the following gifts.

Gift #1:

Listen to audio:
"3 Secrets to Enjoying Early Dates"

http://www.judithjoshel.com/special-bonus-1/

Gift #2:

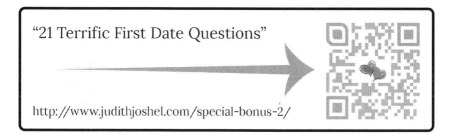

"21 Terrific First Date Questions"

http://www.judithjoshel.com/special-bonus-2/

Contents

Acknowledgements

I want to thank all the women who shared their stories about meeting Mr. Right in the videos, stories, advice and quotes throughout this book. Your contributions have brought the book alive.

I also want to thank my truly awesome mentor, Dr. Diana Kirschner, author of "Love in 90 Days" and creator of the powerful Love Mentoring program which helps women and men of all ages bring lasting love into their lives. Her training and wise supervision have been an invaluable blessing. I also want to thank Dr. Diana's awesome group of Love Mentors who have generously shared their support and wisdom.

I wish to thank all of my former and current clients who have taught me so much about how to help women find and keep Mr. Right. It has been my privilege and pleasure to work with each of them.

I want to thank my awesome coaches Rachael Jayne and Datta Groover. I am especially grateful to Rachael Jayne for her clarity and inspiration on the importance of keeping your attention focused and your mindset in tune with your higher self and purpose above all else. And to Datta, a true renaissance man, for his grounded practicality, empathy and humor and his steady support of my progress.

I also want to thank my awesome book marketing coach, Tamara Monosoff. Tamara has always been ready to answer all my questions just as soon as I ask them and to support the completion and marketing of my book in all ways. She is a treasure.

A special thanks goes to my brilliant editor, Marilyn Levy. Marilyn immediately understood and supported my mission in this book and made innumerable valuable suggestions for improvement, both big and small. Besides being a brilliant editor and writer, Marilyn is a therapist who understands the struggles of women who want to meet Mr. Right.

And thanks to my girlfriends who listened patiently when I talked about the challenges of writing this book and who were always there for support and encouragement.

Most of all I want to deeply appreciate the patience and support of my own Mr. Right husband, who put up with my obsessive work schedule and who was always there to add humor and perspective and to help me whenever I needed help. He is an exacting critic and I am very proud that he loves the book.

Message to My Readers

This book is interactive! Bring it to life. All the QR (Quick Response) codes throughout the book can be scanned with your Smartphone or iPad to watch the videos that were created especially for you.

The women featured here all met their husbands or significant others in the real world. Each of the videos is approximately two minutes long. You will see that at least some of these lovely women are just like you. I have included their stories to inspire you and give you hope on your journey to your Mr. Right.

How to Scan the QR Codes in This Book

Step 1: Download a *free* QR code reader onto your smartphone by searching the App Store.

Step 2: Tap the app once it has downloaded to your phone; this will open up the Reader. Tap again, and your camera will appear to be on. Hover over the code you wish to scan, and the camera will automatically take a picture of the QR code; then your phone will be directed to the respective web page on judithjoshel.com that contains each video message.

Enjoy!

Chapter 1
Introduction

(P. 6)

Watch Video Message:
Judith Joshel Introduces Chapter 1

http://www.judithjoshel.com/wagg-chapter-1/

"Where can I meet quality single guys? Do they even exist?" Kate pleaded. "For the last two years, I've tried online dating, dating apps and looking for guys in every other way I can think of, and I just can't seem to find guys I want to date — let alone marry.

Though there are tons of self-help books on love, dating and relationships, "Where Are the Good Guys? The Single Woman's Guide to Meeting Mr. Right *Offline*" addresses those of you who are tired of online dating or who don't want to do it at all, or who want to continue with online dating while learning ways to meet good guys offline. My book offers incredible, tried and true suggestions about how to meet quality guys in the real world. There are suggestions for women of all ages and of all backgrounds and interests. Included are more suggestions than anyone could use in one lifetime. As a love, dating and relationship coach for women, it's my job to offer advice specifically meant for them — and for you. So sit down, breathe, and relax. Help is on the way.

We've heard about all the marriages and long-term relationships that have resulted from online dating and most of us know married couples who have met that way. Research studies cited by the media tell us 20 to 35% of all couples who marry these days have met through online dating and apps. Many of my own clients have met their Mr. Right on sites from OKCupid to Tinder to Match.com. But more and more women tell me they're fed up with online dating and want to meet good guys in more natural ways. The question is — how to do this. Jody, a client in her mid-twenties, was speechless when I suggested that she try meeting guys in the real world. Although she had met a few guys she liked in the course of her everyday life, she considered online dating and apps to be **the** way to meet guys. She said she didn't have a clue about where and how to meet single guys offline.

If this describes you, and if you're feeling frustrated with your attempts to meet good guys online, you've come to the right place. You're also in the right place if you don't want to try online dating at all. In fact, the idea of online dating and apps may scare you — but you don't know how to meet available men any other way. Although I do encourage women to use various ways to meet guys, including online dating, I've helped many women create strategies to meet great guys offline, and those strategies have worked amazingly well.

This book is for you if:

- You're frustrated and discouraged with online dating;

- You don't want to try online dating or use a dating app – ever – and you want to meet men only in real world;

  and/or

- You want some powerful strategies to meet men offline while continuing to meet them online.

If you're reading this book, you probably fall into one or more of these categories. My promise to you is this: If you carefully follow a fraction of my suggestions, you will start meeting more single men. And some of these men are bound to be quality guys. Your opportunities will, of course, be magnified if you look and feel your best and if you know how to be warm and welcoming to new people.

"Where Are the Good Guys?" begins with some general rules about changing the ways you've chosen to meet men. Then I'll suggest tons of specific ideas on where to go and what to do to meet quality guys. You probably won't be able to use all of these ideas because there are just too many. But a number of them will appeal to you, and I challenge you to choose some of them and to make a concrete plan to put them into action.

"Where Are the Good Guys" is like a puzzle. You can put the pieces together in any order, just as you can read this book in any order. Eventually, you'll come out with a complete picture — hopefully a picture of you the bride and your Mr. Right walking down that proverbial aisle.

My guess is, however, that you'll read some of the later chapters first, as they contain specific ideas about where to meet good men. That's great! Take some of the ideas and put them into action right now. I'd be delighted if you did that. But I also hope that you actually study the general rules and concepts I discuss in Chapters 2 through 7. These rules and concepts are relatively simple and following them will change the way you show up in your life. They'll make you more visible and magnetic to everyone you come into contact with, including quality available men.

I was single for many years and met men in all sorts of ways — some conventional and some not. I met guys simply walking around my neighborhood. I met several boyfriends at parties. I met a long-term boyfriend while walking my cat in a remote area of the park. I've met guys on planes and trains. I met a great boyfriend while doing volunteer work. I've met good guys through classical ads and online too — on match.com and on Craigslist of all places. And I met a number of very high quality men, including my husband, through girlfriends.

My clients, too, have met quality men in all sorts of ways. One recently met a man she's crazy about while walking her dog in her neighborhood. Another reconnected with an old platonic male friend at a bar mitzvah, and now they're talking long term. Another met the love of her life after just a month on match.com.

I'm here to tell you that there are opportunities to meet good single men everywhere. But you need to get yourself out in the world with your eyes open, ~~looking and~~ feeling good.

To be successful, you may first have to address your own way of thinking and behaving and your specific mindset about meeting men.

Chapter 2
Your Mindset:
How You Show Up in the World

Watch Video Message:
Judith Joshel Introduces Chapter 2

http://www.judithjoshel.com/wagg-chapter-2/

How you think about men will greatly affect the ease or difficulty you have in finding quality guys to date. Our mindsets and our thought patterns profoundly affect how we experience reality. I am sure that many of you agree, especially if you are spiritually and psychologically aware. But I have found that even the most spiritually aware women often are not aware of their negative mindsets concerning men and how it affects their love lives. Or they may be aware of some occasional negative feelings and thoughts about men, but they aren't aware of how their negative thoughts and feelings affect their ability to attract good men. In other words, they believe that possessing awareness is enough. **Although awareness is crucial, it's just the beginning of the process.** You must not only catch these negative thoughts and feelings when they arise, you must also challenge them each time, **and** keep yourself from expressing them through your words and behavior. This is easier said than done, but it absolutely can be done. Many of my clients have successfully done it — and the results have been incredible.

I'll be specific. Do you believe there are very few or even no good available men out there? Do you believe there are no good available men you would be attracted to and/or who would be attracted to you? Do you believe that all or most of the available men are second-rate, have something seriously wrong with them, are untrustworthy and/or are liars and cheaters? If you believe any of these things, I'm here to tell you that they aren't true. Sure, some guys are dreadful, but many others are terrific. There may not be hundreds of quality available men if you live in a rural area, but you'd be surprised just how many there are if you keep an open mind. If you live in or near an urban area, available men are everywhere.

I have noticed that many women who want to meet Mr. Right focus on meeting guys for just a limited amount of time each week. For instance, during a week they may go to a party or maybe out to a bar or another social activity with friends. And while at the party or out with friends, they're looking for guys to meet. That's a start, but if you really want to meet your Mr. Right, your best chance to connect with him is to be **open to the possibility of meeting him during every waking hour of your life.** To do this, you need to nurture what I call your **Man Radar** and to keep it on.

I can almost hear you saying, "How can I possibly do that, Judith? My life is very busy. I'm a career woman, and I have other obligations as well — to my kids, to my frail parents, to my friends, to my church, and so on."

I totally get it. Your life is over-the-top busy — and you may feel overwhelmed — at least some of the time — with everything that's on your plate. Not so many years ago, I was in that same place — running my law practice, caring for my elderly mother, trying to stay healthy and positive, trying to take good care of myself and on top of it all trying to meet my Mr. Right.

Since your very busy life seriously limits the amount of time and energy you have to devote solely to meeting men, I invite you to examine your beliefs on where you might meet good guys. If I told you that there are possibilities of meeting good available guys absolutely everywhere, I wonder what you'd say. My guess is something like this: "But Judith, I almost never see attractive men in my daily life. And attractive men rarely if ever approach me." And I would respond that I believe you, but I think you're wearing blinders.

We all tend to operate wearing blinders. By that I mean that we limit our perceptions; we see only what we expect ourselves to see based on our past experiences and our mindset. Say you decide to buy a new car. You notice cars on the road you haven't looked at carefully before. When you decide which model you want — a Honda Accord, for instance — you start noticing all the Honda Accords on the road. Suddenly, you become aware that there are lots of Honda Accords around — many more than you've ever dreamed possible. This happens to me every time I decide to re-place my car. As soon as I decide the kind of car I want, I start seeing that car everywhere.

It's the same with men. If you go about your daily life with the at-titude that there are lots of available men out there, you will start noticing possibilities you were blind to before. But in order to shift your mindset and to start noticing attractive men in your daily en-vironment, you need to make three changes.

First and foremost, you need to take your eyes off your phone and your tablet. Put these wonderful addictive devices away whenever you're in a public space. There are two reasons why. With your nose buried in your smartphone or your iPad, you won't notice much of what's around you. The most gorgeous guy may be standing behind you in line at Starbucks, and you won't notice him. Even worse, if that gorgeous guy notices you and wants to make a connection, he won't do it if your eyes are glued to your phone. He won't want to interrupt you; he has no reason to think that you might be receptive to a friendly remark. Guys are ex-pected to initiate with women, but even the most attractive ones get rejected a lot. I'm sure you hate being rejected. Guys hate it too. No guy wants to put himself out there if he thinks you're go-ing to reject him.

Second, shift your mindset to a state I call **Radically Open Curi-osity**. Someone with Radically Open Curiosity will try to be fully present in the moment all the time. For example, if you're in a mindset of Radically Open Curiosity on your way to work, you'll notice everything around you — from your neighbor also heading out to work, to the new snow on the ground, as you walk to your car, to the sunny or cloudy or rainy weather, to the people in line at the coffee shop. You get the idea. You're forming a new habit, but it takes practice to get the hang of it. Begin by trying to notice whenever you're in your head — when you're wrapped up in your thoughts and worries — and call yourself back to the present. Remind yourself to be present with all your senses — to see and hear and feel and sense everyone and everything around you.

This is actually a challenging practice. We tend to be in our heads a lot — thinking our many thoughts, worrying about our problems, planning our day and so on. Radically Open Curiosity challenges you to stay in a state of awareness and receptivity as much as possible. This is really good for us, not only in terms of meeting men, but because when we're in this state of Radically Open Curiosity, we are truly present and alive. And we're open to experiences and encounters we might otherwise miss if our focus is on all the thoughts and worries in our head and the feelings in our bodies.

However, I caution you not to be self-critical. Even people adept at meditation, sometimes slip into their heads while they're meditating and start worrying about a problem or mentally writing their grocery lists. Staying present and open can even feel awkward at first — as anything does until it becomes habit.

In practicing Radically Open Curiosity on her daily walk, Lori decided to look for things she had never noticed before. One day she saw some lovely gold colored roses that had never caught her eye. The next day she heard the calls of an unfamiliar bird and she encountered a friendly grey cat who approached her to be petted. On the third day she saw the delivery of a new refrigerator to her neighbor's home and passed some kids drawing on the sidewalk with colored chalk. Her walks had become so interesting that she looked forward to being surprised by something new each day. After a couple weeks, this new way of approaching her walk began to feel more and more natural, and by the end of a month, Lori's mindset of Radically Open Curiosity on her daily walks had become automatic. It had become a part of her life — just as Radically Open Curiosity can in time become a natural part of your life.

Third and finally, we want to add to our Radically Open Curiosity mindset an attitude of warm friendliness. This means that you're ready to smile at and greet the people you see in your daily life. When you're moving through life every day in the state of Radically Open Curiosity and with a warm friendly attitude, I guarantee that you'll start noticing people you've never noticed before, you'll become more visible to people around you, and you'll start making casual connections with a lot of people. Over time some of them will be available quality men as well as people who know good available men to whom they might introduce you.

There are lots and lots of great single guys who'd love to meet a wonderful catch like you. Some of them are actively looking for a girlfriend online and elsewhere. But what about those guys who aren't actively looking, but would dearly love to meet Ms. Right? A quality available guy will immediately notice a confident woman who is practicing Radically Open Curiosity and who makes eye contact with him, smiles and says hi. And if he's interested, or even just curious, your way of being in the world will give him permission to talk to you and maybe eventually ask you out. Sure, it won't happen every time, but it will happen more often than you think.

Think of yourself as an available taxi. Keep your green light on.

I get that being open, curious, warm and friendly will be a real challenge for some of you. If you are by nature an introvert like me, you may be drawn into yourself a lot of the time. You may feel shy and uncomfortable about giving people you don't know a smile and a hi. But I won't let you off the hook just because you're not naturally extraverted — and try not to let yourself off the hook, either. Your natural way of being in the world is fine, but it will make meeting guys offline much more difficult than it needs to be.

Start experimenting with a Radically Open Curiosity mindset and a warm and friendly attitude for short periods of time. Try practicing, for instance, only on your way to work or just on your lunch break or just during a trip to the grocery store. At first, focus on giving a warm friendly smile to women, to children, to men who are too old or too young for you. Gradually you'll become more comfortable with this new way of being in the world and you'll feel less and less intimidated by being friendly to attractive guys.

It still may feel scary, but that's ok. Remind yourself that breaking old comfortable patterns that don't serve you is always challenging. Things that are truly worth doing are often difficult and quite uncomfortable at first. But if you're willing to face your discomfort, if only for 10 or 15 minutes a day at the beginning, this way of being in the world will start to feel natural and even really good to you.

My client Bethany is accomplished in her career, but she's shy about talking to strangers. I gave her the challenge of engaging in a short conversation with a stranger every day. The pharmacy clerk and the bus driver counted. Although there were days Bethany didn't do this, on most days she did. One day there were two cute guys standing beside her on the bus home from work who were discussing their local baseball team's chances of winning the game that night. It so happened that Bethany followed the team and she challenged herself to make a comment about the pitcher for the game. She got into an animated conversation with these guys and one of them, Evan, asked her to go with him to a game the next Saturday afternoon. She accepted, had a great time, and they have been dating exclusively for about 6 months.

Chapter 3
Strategies for Meeting Men

Watch Video Message:
Judith Joshel Introduces Chapter 3

http://www.judithjoshel.com/wagg-chapter-3/

Some of the strategies I suggest for meeting men are quite broad. They target places where lots of men gather and activities in which many men participate. For example, lots of men can be found in sports bars watching Monday Night Football and tons of men attend car shows. Many different types of men will be there. You may be interested in some of them, but you may have nothing in common with many of them. Still, the possibilities exist. My client Monique met her fiancée at a high-end sports bar and my friend's daughter Trina met her husband at the International Auto Show in Atlanta. Trina was car, not man shopping at the time. She went to the auto show to check out several cars she might be interested in buying. Jeff was checking out some Nissan models and started a conversation with Trina who was also checking out Nissans. They spent the rest of the afternoon together exploring the auto show and then went out to dinner together. After a two-year courtship, they are now happily married

In contrast to the broad strategies I suggest, other strategies for meeting guys are narrower and more concentrated, focusing on places where men with specific interests can be found and activities in which men with specific interests participate. For example, a guy who's an animal lover and enjoys doing volunteer work might be found training dogs for the blind, deaf and disabled or rescuing and caring for injured wildlife. If you have a passion for helping animals and would simply love to find a caring man who shares that passion, you might want to volunteer at a school that trains service dogs or at a wildlife refuge center. You'd probably love doing this work, and you just might meet that wonderful right guy who shares your love for animals and your desire to be of service. Brianne is passionate about dogs. She volunteered a couple hours a week at Southeastern Guide Dogs on the Florida Gulf Coast, helping to socialize puppies and walk young dogs being trained to help disabled veterans. While there walking dogs, she met Bill, another volunteer and they started walking their assigned dogs together. Their relationship turned into a romance. Today they are married with three dogs of their own. They actively support a dog-training organization near their home.

Later, in this book I share hundreds of places and activities where you might meet quality guys. I suggest that you experiment with a number of them. Try a few of the wide strategies and also some narrower strategies focusing on the kinds of interests and values you'd love your Mr. Right to have. Experiment. Have fun. If you don't meet anyone interesting the first time, don't immediately write off that venue or activity. I'd be rich if I had a dollar for each time a client told me she didn't want to go to a certain venue or participate in a certain activity — because she'd already been there, done that. Why not try the venue or activity at least another time or two? Just because you didn't meet an interesting guy the first time, doesn't mean your experience the second or third time will be the same. Try it again. If you went to a meetup hike and didn't meet anyone, but you enjoyed the hike, try it at least one more time.

My client Amber met Roger, the guy she married, on the fourth bike ride she attended with the same meetup group. She'd met no guys who had interested her on her first three meetup rides. But on the fourth ride, she met Roger when she joined the meetup group for lunch after the ride. Roger had been recently divorced and was not really ready for a committed relationship. But he was drawn to Amber, and they started to date, often going as a couple on group bike rides. Within a year, they were engaged and are now happily married with a 2-year-old daughter.

Amber didn't give up on the meetup bike rides because she also loved bike riding, and because the riding itself made her feel better, physically and mentally. So before saying, "Been there, done that and I'm not going back," remember Amber.

Everywhere you go, I challenge you to consider if it might be a good venue for meeting guys. Some of the best places for meeting men are open environments where people gather for common reasons or interests and where they expect to meet new people. Examples are: festivals, fairs, outdoor concerts, neighborhood block parties, improvisation classes, wedding receptions, and political rallies.

Waiting rooms and lines are great places to strike up conversations with strangers. When you're in a waiting room at a doctor's office or in your dentist's waiting room dreading your upcoming appointment, when you're at a car repair shop or a car wash, be on the lookout for men and make a casual comment when you can. That cute guy who's also waiting might just be interested in you.

The same thing goes when you find yourself in line — whether at Starbucks, the grocery store, a bus stop or a local food truck. There may be a guy standing near you. If he looks interesting, why not smile and say something — anything? You can ask him a question; guys often love to answer questions and solve problems. If he finds you attractive and he's available, he'll try to keep the conversation going. If he doesn't respond, don't take it personally. He may have a girlfriend or a wife, may simply be having a bad day or may be preoccupied about something completely unrelated to you. It's not personal. Many women assume that if a guy doesn't respond, it's their fault — they aren't attractive enough, the guy sees them as too aggressive or awkward or something else is wrong with the way they are coming across. Never make assumptions about why a guy doesn't respond to your smile or friendly comment. The reason is likely to be completely unrelated to you.

When you're dating and looking for guys to date, you'll sometimes reject guys and sometimes you'll be rejected — often for no good reason it may seem. That's part of the dating game. If you want to meet your Mr. Right, you have to take that risk. And always remember that any guy who shows interest in you is also taking the risk that you won't be interested in him. If you're willing to take that risk, you might fail to achieve what you want. But if you don't take a risk you can be 100% sure you won't get it. So try to cultivate a light attitude and a thick skin. Go slow and give yourself some time to get to know a guy. Don't get heavily invested in any particular guy too quickly no matter how perfect for you he seems. Realize that he may be great, but he may not. Your job is to learn about him and find out whether he's the right man for you. Then if he disappears early on as sometimes happens or acts badly in another way, you'll be disappointed, but your heart won't be broken, and you'll pick yourself up and continue to meet new men.

Chapter 4
Be Open to Going Alone

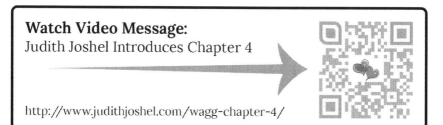

Watch Video Message:
Judith Joshel Introduces Chapter 4

http://www.judithjoshel.com/wagg-chapter-4/

Many women I speak with are reluctant to go to places or join activities alone, even though they might meet single men there. Some won't go alone under any condition. If you feel this way, I get it, but you're likely shooting yourself in the foot.

I understand how difficult going out alone is. None of your girlfriends may be interested in going to a paddle-boarding meetup with you, or they simply may not be available when you want to go out. You may not have any unattached girlfriends, and married women friends might find it impossible to get away. So the bottom line is if you won't go alone, you won't go at all.

But let's look at the situation from a different perspective. You may believe that going with a girlfriend or two will give you more confidence, but once you get to your destination, it may give you less confidence. Your girlfriend might attract all the male attention while you stand in her shadow feeling like you're hidden under Harry Potter's invisibility cloak.

Or maybe you're the one who attracts guys easily and being with a girlfriend or two makes you feel more confident about going out. You may feel good about how magnetic you are to men in comparison to your girlfriend, but you may also feel a bit guilty and kind of sorry for her because you know she can't be feeling terrific when you're getting all the male attention.

Also – when you're with a girlfriend or two, many men will feel shyer and more self conscious about approaching you than they would if you were alone. A man might not even risk approaching you at all because he knows you might reject him, and it's a lot harder to be rejected in front of an audience than in a one on one encounter. I've coached a number of guys and you have no idea how scary it can be for a guy to approach an attractive woman. Even the most awesome guys get regularly rejected. Why make it so much harder for an amazing guy to approach you by surrounding yourself with girlfriends?

If you won't go to venues or activities by yourself, even though you might meet interesting single men, you are seriously limiting your opportunities to meet guys. I have known educated women with great jobs who will never go out to dinner alone — and some won't go out alone for lunch or breakfast either. Just think about how profoundly restricting this fear of doing things on your own will be for your life experiences. I had this fear when I was younger. But I worked hard on overcoming it, because I could see how it controlled and constricted my life. I was able to conquer my fear, and you can too if you're determined to do it.

Let's take just a moment to consider why women in particular fear going alone to activities. It often has to do with fearing the judgments of others — She's eating dinner by herself in a restaurant. What's wrong with her? The fact is that most people don't even notice you dining alone, and most who do have zero negative judgments about you. And if someone does judge you for eating alone in a restaurant, so what? Why does a stranger's judgment matter? That judgment, in fact, says more about him or her than it says about you. If you find yourself judging single women sitting alone at a table, challenge yourself to let go of that judgment.

Make a commitment to yourself to ratchet up your courage. I suggest going alone to an activity or event you already know you'll enjoy. Go with the sole intention of having fun and being friendly. Give yourself permission to leave early if you want to, but even if you leave early, give yourself lots of points for having had the courage to go. You don't have to speak to guys if you feel too insecure and nervous. Just go, participate and be friendly to women. And then keep challenging yourself by continuing to go alone to different venues and activities.

I do everything alone.

Each week challenge yourself to do something by yourself that you would normally never do alone. Start with something like lunch by yourself in a new restaurant or a short visit to a street fair. Then try some meetup groups that really interest you. It doesn't matter whether they are groups that would particularly attract men. Just go and be friendly with the intention of having a good time. As you become more comfortable, challenge yourself to go to activities and places where single men are likely to be. Go on a group bike ride or take an investment seminar or a photography class.

Give yourself a little reward at the end of every day when you've made an effort to communicate. If you've talked to a guy in the dentist's office, that counts. And when you've made contact with one guy every day for a month, give yourself a bigger reward. This actually works scientifically, because it changes your neurological impulses – your mindset.

Lots and lots of couples have met at events and activities to which each had gone alone. My Facebook friend Timi went to a large outdoor concert by herself and she met the man she married in the parking lot. Their cars were parked nose to nose. Another couple I know met at a bike festival. My friend Elaine met her long-term boyfriend at a painting class. The possibilities are limitless! And if you go alone and are warm and welcoming, it's so much easier for guys to approach you than it would be if you're surrounded by a group of girlfriends.

Chapter 5
How You Feel about How You Look

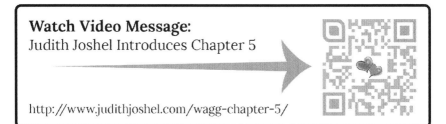

Watch Video Message:
Judith Joshel Introduces Chapter 5

http://www.judithjoshel.com/wagg-chapter-5/

How do you feel about the way you look? This is an important question if you want to attract Mr. Right. A number of women have actually said things like this to me, "The emphasis on female beauty today is ridiculous. I am who I am, and I'm not going to change my appearance for any man. If a guy doesn't like me for who I am, then so be it. It makes me angry that men judge women by their physical appearance, and I'm not going to play that game."

I agree that our culture's emphasis on female sexiness and beauty is out of control and can cause real problems for girls, adolescents and grown women. I also believe that it's important for women and men to show up as our best selves in all parts of our life including our love lives. The thing is, if you want to attract quality men, you need to feel like a quality woman. Part of feeling like a quality woman is feeling good about your looks. I am not saying that you have to look like a gorgeous sexy bombshell in order to find your soul mate. I just want you to look good for your age, weight and body type and most important to feel good about the way you look. If you run around doing errands on Saturday in old unflattering sweatpants without a touch of makeup, you probably won't be feeling very attractive, let alone feminine or sexy. If you aren't feeling very attractive or sexy, you won't be putting your best foot forward if you happen to run into a guy in the grocery store who may be a great match for you.

Let's pull this apart. There's you and how you're feeling about

WHERE ARE THE GOOD GUYS?

yourself and there's him and whether he's feeling attracted to you. It's a fact that men are visual creatures. We may not like that, but men are wired that way. When you're out in the world not feeling great about the way you look, you're not putting out confident and magnetic energy that tends to draw men toward you. If you're serious about meeting the right guy, why not take the time and effort to look and feel good about the way you look before going out into the world? Yes, I know. You're busy and you really don't have time for this. If you're feeling that way much of the time, I invite you to take a deeper look and see if there's anything more profound that might be going on. When I've given this assignment to clients, several have realized that they don't want to look too attractive or sexy because they've had some bad or even terrifying experiences with men when they were younger, sometimes even when they were children. Although they really want a committed relationship with a man who treasures them, they may also be scared of men, especially at first. So not looking their most attractive can make them feel safe from unwanted male attention. The problem is that they may also be protecting themselves so completely that their perfect Mr. Right may walk right past them.

If experiences from your past trigger fears that may be preventing you from moving forward, you may want to consider consulting a therapist to help you move on and enable you to accept your best self.

When I was dating, I took serious stock of my physical assets and liabilities and took steps to enhance my attractive features and to minimize my liabilities. If you're really serious about finding your Mr. Right, I suggest that you do the same. There are makeover consultants who can give you invaluable advice on your hair, makeup and clothes. Or you can address this on your own as I did. Find a great hair stylist and see what she suggests. You can get makeup makeovers at department stores' makeup counters. Use the tips you like and leave the rest. You don't have to buy any products you're not sure about. Go to a clothing store with savvy saleswomen and find one to suggest clothing styles and colors that are flattering for you. Once you get a sense of the styles and colors that look best on you, you can go anywhere to buy clothes.

Wearing the right colors for your complexion and your eyes, especially near your face, will help you look more alive and radiant. On the other hand, wearing the wrong colors can make you look sallow or grey and dull your complexion. If you've never paid much attention to how different colors look on you, try this. Gather clothing and scarves in a number of different colors. Stand in front of a well-lit mirror and hold each garment under your chin. Pay close attention to how each color affects your skin tone and radiance. A color that is right for you will light up your face. A color that isn't right for you will make your skin look dull, sallow or washed out.

If you'd like to have your colors done professionally, a professional wardrobe or makeup consultant may be able to help you. Or google "personal color analysis consultants." You can also find online sites for help on determining your best colors by googling "my personal colors." Many women have found the book "Color Me Beautiful" by Carole Jackson helpful. I applaud those women already aware of the power of wearing their best colors. If you haven't really considered this before, you may be amazed at how changes in the colors of your clothing affect the way you look and how you feel about how you look.

If you want to lose weight, do it. It often really helps to get support from Weight Watchers or a similar program. Your doctor may have suggestions.

Believe me, if you have a positive open mindset, a friendly attitude and feel that you're looking good, you will be well on your way to meeting the love of your life.

What if you are often told that you are very pretty or even amazingly beautiful and you attract men easily, but they are the wrong kind of guys or they are good guys, but you can't seem to hold their interest? You would probably be shocked at the number of truly beautiful women I've coached who have experienced these problems. These women sometimes come across as cold, inauthentic or needy. There are many possible reasons for this and they are beyond the scope of this book. But if you relate to what I've just said, you would likely benefit from working with a therapist or with a coach who is trained to work on a deep level.

On the opposite end of the spectrum are women I've known who are not conventionally attractive, but who are intensely attractive to men. A woman comes to mind who by American standards would be considered overweight and quite unattractive. However, when she walks, she carries herself like a ballerina. She's incredibly confident, outgoing and friendly, warm and gracious. She dresses well, and her makeup is impeccable. A musician with a positive sense of herself and her value, she's married to an attractive man who's even more accomplished than she is. And he adores her. There are many many women who are not conventionally attractive, but who have great relationships with terrific guys who dearly love them. If you are not happy with your appearance, by all means take steps to improve it. But always remember there's truth in the saying, "Beauty is only skin deep." Although you may not be conventionally beautiful, if you are willing to be warm, open and authentic, you are likely to attract an amazing partner.

Chapter 6
How You Feel about How He Looks

Watch Video Message:
Judith Joshel Introduces Chapter 6

http://www.judithjoshel.com/wagg-chapter-6/

Are you extremely particular about the guys you date? Do you re-ject guys who satisfy at least some of your requirements because they aren't your physical type and/or you don't feel chemistry? Do you want him to have the right education, the perfect career and the right style of clothes? Does he need to be outgoing and social? Does he have to be tall and in top physical shape? If you've said yes to any of these questions, you may be seriously crippling your chance to find your perfect guy.

You may have a specific picture of how your Mr. Right will be – and you may be dead wrong. Here is a surprising fact: many wom-en in very happy and fulfilling marriages were not at first attracted to the guy they ended up marrying. I did an informal survey of about 100 happily married women I know and found that about one-third of them fell into this category.

My advice to my clients is to be open to dating and getting to know a variety of men. That's the purpose of dating — to get to know a number of men so that you can find the one who is right for you. You may think you will know that very soon after you meet a guy, but you're probably fooling yourself. Men are as complicated as we are, and it takes time to get to know them. There's no way to get around it. Of course, you need to have chemistry with the man you marry. But chemistry isn't always instant. It sometimes devel-ops as you get to know a guy and learn how amazing he is. If he is really interested in you and treats you like gold, if there are things you like about him, if he shows himself to be trustworthy and kind, and if you feel at least neutral about his looks, date him a few times, be open, get to know him. If by the 4th or 5th date, you still feel no attraction, I'll let you off the hook. You can tell him that you think he's great, but you don't think the two of you are a match. Until then, keep an open mind and give him a chance. It may sound counterintuitive, but having this attitude will actually speed up your path to Mr. Right.

Chapter 7
Lighten Up!

Watch Video Message:
Judith Joshel Introduces Chapter 7

http://www.judithjoshel.com/wagg-chapter-7/

"After God created the world, He made man and woman. Then, to keep the whole thing from collapsing, He invented humor."

— Bill Kelly

If you are willing to take your dating experiences lightly, you will be doubly blessed. Not only are you likely to meet your Mr. Right sooner rather than later, you will have lots of fun along the way. A sense of humor will make all the difference to your dating success. Look at it this way; dating to find your Mr. Right is one of life's great adventures. You get to meet amazing guys who may have led amazing lives. Some will be amazingly sexy and others amazingly unattractive. Some will be amazingly interesting and others amazingly boring. You get the picture. Think of this as a big adventure. You can make that adventure the most extraordinary ride of your life, or you can make it a tense and fearful ride. It's your choice.

When you see a new guy you'd like to meet, be curious. Ask yourself, "How can I attract him? How can I connect with him?" If your interaction or lack of interaction with him doesn't result in a date, ask yourself if there's anything you might have done differently, anything you might change in your attitude and behavior that might result in a date next time.

If the two of you connect and he's asked you out, stop yourself from obsessing on the fruitless question, "Is he the one?" Just have a good time on the date — no more, no less. Be curious about what he's like, if he's fun, if he's interesting. And try not to be judgmental. He may be nervous, whether or not he shows it.

Odd and ridiculous things sometimes happen when you're dating.

My friend Trisha has one of the world's greatest senses of humor. She dated for many years after her divorce before she met her beloved Bill and had a number of very funny experiences along the way. One guy talked about himself for over 2 hours straight on a first date without asking Trisha one question about herself and without noticing that her eyes had glazed over about 30 minutes into the date. On their way out of the restaurant, he turned to Trisha and casually asked, "You're a nurse, aren't you?" "Something like that," she replied and made a beeline for her car. Trisha is an investment banker.

My friend Mary remembers going on a first date with a guy who brought along his pet raccoon. They were headed to a nearby hiking trail. Mary was driving. The raccoon got loose, climbed under the dashboard and proceeded to chew the wires until Mary's date could get him under control. There was no second date.

On one of my first dates in college I spilled an entire hot fudge sundae into my lap. To this day I have no idea how that happened. I was mortified, but also relieved, because I was bored to tears and wanted to end the date and go home. I now had the perfect excuse.

Hallie, an acquaintance, told me this story. One Thursday night when she was in college, the washing machine where she lived was on the fritz and she desperately needed clean clothes for work on Friday. It was after 11 when she arrived at the laundromat. She loaded her clothes into four machines, added detergent, placed quarters in the money slots, pressed start, and nothing happened. Hallie was puzzled and looked to see if the washers were plugged in. They were. In the meantime, a good looking guy had come into the laundromat and was watching Hallie's dilemma. Without a word, he walked over to the washing machines and put more quarters in the money slots. The machines started. He never said a word, but went next door to a café and brought back coffee for himself and a hot chocolate for Hallie. They sipped their drinks and chatted while their clothes were being washed and dried. The guy, whose name is Larry, carried Hallie's laundry to her car, and they said goodbye. Although her washing machine had been repaired, Hallie returned to the laundromat the following Thursday night in hopes of seeing Larry again. She threw her clothes in washers, started them easily this time, and waited for what seemed like forever. As she was about to load the dryers, Larry pulled up. Before he entered the laundromat, Hallie quickly tossed her wet clean clothes back into the washing machines, started the machines, grabbed a magazine and sat down to compose herself. Larry came in, said hi, loaded a few washing machines and sat down with his newspaper. Then he went next door and brought back coffee for himself and hot chocolate for Hallie. They chatted easily and Larry shared a story that showed his strength of character and depth. Hallie was impressed. This was the start of a romance and a happy 30 year marriage. Years later Hallie aired her dirty laundry and came clean with Larry about her laundry ruse. Now there's a creative woman. She had met a promising guy, but did not want to leave their future meeting to chance. Ask yourself if there is there something here you can learn from Hallie.

We're not the only ones who have weird and funny first date experiences. Men have them too. My old friend Brian was in his early 20s and interested in a beautiful woman who worked with and loved exotic animals. When he arrived to pick her up for their first date, she invited him in to wait while she finished getting ready. He was shocked and unnerved. Her home was filled with large and small exotic animals, most of them not in cages. There was a huge snake slithering around. Then a large black bird swooped over his head onto the living room light fixture. Brian is an animal lover, but he's more a cat and dog guy with a tolerance for rabbits and small fish. All he could think of was running out of the apartment, never to return. Though he forced himself to stay until his date was ready, he remembers nothing more about this date. Beautiful and interesting as this woman was, there was no second date.

To get the most fun out of dating and to remain enthusiastic about meeting Mr. Right after interacting with so many Mr. Wrongs, I recommend that you consciously cultivate an attitude of openness, curiosity and amusement. Try keeping a journal of your funny and weird dating adventures. You might even decide to publish that journal one day. Consider Wendy Newman whose book "121 First Dates" became a bestseller. She had some pretty great and some pretty outrageous first dates. Wendy's secret is that she maintained her sense of humor through it all and kept meeting new men until she finally met the wonderful guy she married. This can happen to you too if you refuse to give up and continue to put your best self forward. So why not nurture your curiosity and your sense of humor and enjoy your journey?

Caveat. It's easy for your sense of humor about your weird dating experiences to turn into man bashing. Man bashing is not helpful. Your last date may have been an astonishingly clueless weirdo, but your next one may be Mr. Right. If you're in a man bashing frame of mind when you meet him, you may very well scare him away. Carry your sense of humor lightly and consciously clear out the negative thoughts and feelings about your last disappointing date before meeting a new guy. Talking about past dates is a definite no-no. At least until you have a committed relationship with Mr. Yes. Always remember that the new guy is a COMPLETELY different person from any guy you've ever known. He deserves a warm, open and nonjudgmental welcome from you.

Chapter 8
Networking

Watch Video Message:
Judith Joshel Introduces Chapter 8

http://www.judithjoshel.com/wagg-chapter-8/

I am certain you know that networking can be very effective in helping you find a job and get ahead in your career. It's also an amazingly effective way to meet quality guys. Years before online dating sites and dating apps came on the scene, networking was a common way to meet quality guys. And here's a little secret – it still is! When I was dating in my 20's, networking was how several of my girlfriends met their husbands. One married the brother of her college friend. Another was fixed up with a male friend of her close girlfriend. In some communities, women routinely introduce their girlfriends to single guys who might be good matches for them. In other communities, this isn't routinely done. But even if you live in such a community, people who like you will often be happy to introduce you to a good guy they know if you're willing to ask.

Here are some good networking ideas:

Friends and Relatives –

Friends and relatives are often a wonderful source of readily available men. They may even be guys you know about or know slightly, whom you may not have found attractive at first glance. In my experience, they frequently turn out to be great, and those guys can make the best husbands.

My eye-popping friend Tina met her husband Ken through their mutual friend, Jenny. They'd already met casually a few times at parties. He was clearly interested in her, but she had no interest in him. He wasn't her physical type. (Her first three husbands were her type physically, but they had other problems. Hence, she had three ex-husbands.) Reluctantly, Tina agreed to exchange texts with Ken, after Jenny suggested that she had nothing to lose. She might even enjoy Ken's company, and they might wind up being friends. Even more reluctantly, Tina went out with Ken when he contacted her. And they did become friends. Good friends. Months later, she realized that Ken was the kindest, most gentle man she'd ever met. Eventually, she happily agreed to marry him — with no reluctance. They've been married for 15 years.

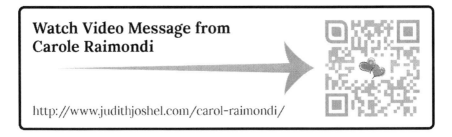

Watch Video Message from Carole Raimondi

http://www.judithjoshel.com/carol-raimondi/

Carole Raimondi is a former tap dancer turned legal advocate for children caught in the middle of their parents' high conflict custody cases. Determined to find joy in her everyday mundane life, she is grateful to have found a loving companion and partner for her retired years. They travel the world together, but live separately the rest of the year.

I got fixed up. In my early 60's. I went to an event with some friends and a man was there who was the boss of one of the women I knew. We talked and he was very nice. He wasn't someone I was terribly interested in other than pleasant conversation. But I got a phone call a couple days later from one of the women saying, "Are you interested in him?" I said, "Well, maybe, but he's gay." There was something about his soft-spokenness and we talked about gardens, and I made an assumption — very bad gaydar! But the two sisters invited us to a family event and we hit it off fantastically. We went back and forth a little bit with emails. He lived an hour away from me, but we found that was not bad for our relationship. We saw each other on the weekend and during the week I could do what I wanted and he could do what he wanted. About 5 years into our relationship he moved close to me, about 15 minutes away. We did discuss living together, but both of us are independent people and we like our own time. We come together and we usually have a very pleasant time because we haven't seen each other and we have a lot to talk about. And we travel together and that's great. You know, meeting someone at the other end of your life when you're already a complete person, you're not going to have children, you're not starting out on a career- he was retired and I retired since I've been with him so we have time to do leisure things and fun things. We both have our good health and I feel really blessed that at this time in my life I've met someone who can be a real companion!

Every woman who wants to meet Mr. Right should be networking and that includes you. Here's what I suggest:

- Make as complete a list of all your friends, relatives, coworkers and acquaintances as possible. Don't rush. Come back to your list several times to be sure you've thought of everyone. You can also continue to update your list as you meet new people.

- Go through your list carefully and check the name of each person you feel is a fan of yours.

- Take out your calendar or bring it up online. Each week for the next few months, write in the names of 2 or 3 people you listed above, those who are your fans.

- Then each week contact the 2 or 3 people whose names you've written in your calendar for that week. During a casual conversation, let them know that you'd love to meet a great available guy. Ask if they know anyone who's open to a committed relationship and in whom you might be interested. If the answer is yes — or let me think about it, let them know that you'd love an introduction. Keep it simple — that's all you need to say about meeting guys, but don't forget to first show interest in your friend by asking her about herself. Let the conversation flow naturally. Maybe your friend will ask, "What's up with you?" Any question like that will give you the perfect invitation to make your request.

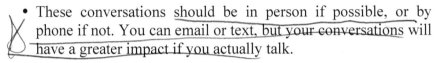

- These conversations should be in person if possible, or by phone if not. You can email or text, but your conversations will have a greater impact if you actually talk.

- If you've never done anything like this, you may feel quite uncomfortable, especially at first. If you do, I suggest that you write out exactly what you want to say and then practice saying it, first in front of a mirror and then in front of a supportive friend until it starts to feel easier.

- If you're feeling nervous, ask yourself why. You may feel ashamed to ask for help finding Mr. Right. You might feel as if there's something wrong with you because you haven't attracted him on your own or that your friends will think there's something wrong with you. But guess what. Most people know it's not always so easy to find the right partner. People who wish the best for you may love to introduce you to any quality available guys whom they know. They won't judge you for being single. My guess is that they'd be over the moon if you hit it off with a guy you've met through them.

Even your grown son or daughter may know a good guy for you. My client Maureen, in her early 50s, was introduced to an attractive guy by her adult daughter. She and her daughter were eating dinner in a local restaurant when two men walked in. One was her daughter's friend and the other was her friend's divorced dad. Maureen and her daughter invited the guys to join them. After dinner, the father — a very attractive man I might add — asked Maureen out.

Acquaintances New and Old –

When you meet someone, in the back of your mind, remember that your new acquaintance just might know the perfect guy for you. If he or she does, they'd probably be happy to introduce you. You just never know. For example, let's say that you go to a meetup hike, but you don't meet any interesting men. You do, however, connect with a woman you like. Think about having coffee or lunch with her after the meetup. The subject of men will probably come up naturally, so why not mention casually that you'd love to meet an awesome unattached guy? If she's single, she probably would, as well, so it won't be awkward to ask if she knows anyone who might be a good match for you. If she does, let her know that you'd so appreciate her putting the two of you in touch. And tell her you'll look out for single guys who might be a good match for her.

If she seems open to your suggestion, give her a business card with your contact information if you have one. If you don't, get some feminine looking cards made. It's very handy to have cards with your contact information ready to give to guys who express an interest and to anyone who might know a good guy for you to meet.

Andrea, one of my clients, met Jane, another single woman, when she decided to try a paddle boarding meetup. Neither had ever paddle boarded before. They both found themselves falling into the water and laughing as they struggled to right themselves. Right away, they had a connection. Later, over breakfast, her new friend told Andrea that she'd love to introduce her to her single brother, who had just moved to town. The rest is history, as they say. Andrea and Jane's brother now have a two-year-old. Jane was the maid of honor at their wedding.

You just never know who will know that right guy for you. One woman told me that the doorman in her building introduced her to the love of her life. Others met men through neighbors, a hairdresser and a manicurist.

Fellow Employees –

Generally, you want to keep your work life and your personal life separate. So think it through carefully before asking a co-worker if he or she knows a guy who'd be a good match for you. What if your co-worker introduced you to her brother, and one of you didn't like the other, or you became a couple and then broke up? If something like this happened, it could negatively affect your relationship with your co-worker whom you see at work every day. I'm not suggesting that you should pass up meeting a co-worker's brother; I'm simply asking you to think about the consequences carefully before you decide.

Alexis' best friend and co-worker fixed her up with her cousin Joe. Joe fell hard for Alexis on their first date, but Alexis didn't return the feeling. Politely, she tried to tell him she didn't think they were a good match. But he continued to pursue her, and her friend kept asking Alexis to give him another chance. Things became more than a little awkward between Alexis and her friend for weeks, both of them upset and trying to avoid each other at the office.

It goes without saying that you'd never want to ask your boss for an introduction — that really would be crossing the line between your work life and personal life.

DJ married a fellow employee. Here's her story:

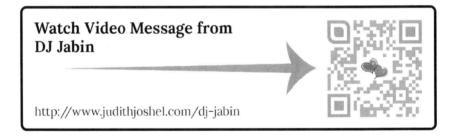

Watch Video Message from DJ Jabin

http://www.judithjoshel.com/dj-jabin

DJ is an author, international speaker, spiritual teacher and transformational guide, supporting individuals and businesses in reaching their highest potential. She is known for her ability to meet people where they are; empowering their transformation by shining a light on the thinking that causes limiting beliefs, struggle or suffering; thereby opening the door to endless creativity.

I have been married for 35 years to the same person. It was very unexpected because I met him at work. His daughter had the measles and I offered to go get her and take care of her. So then I became the go-to girl. Whenever he would go out on dates, he would say, "Hey DJ, do you want to watch Heather? She likes you, you like her." And I'm like, "Sure." And I got to know him and he was such a nice guy. I even said to a friend of mine, "hey, why don't you guys go out because I like him, he's really nice" And I'm telling her about him and I'm like I'm not sure I don't really like him. So here's the deal. I had manifested this person. I wanted these certain things from all the people I'd dated. These were the things that were important to me. For example, I wanted someone who liked the country, loved to be outdoors and at the same time was comfortable going to a ball and dressing up and being in that atmosphere also — being comfortable in both places. I wanted someone who had a willing spirit and who was willing to be adventurous and easy going et cetera. And all these things ended up being in this man who I wasn't necessarily attracted to — not that he wasn't handsome, but he wasn't my typical "type". And so when I realized that, we went on a friend date and we were sitting there in a movie together and I could feel it and he could feel it and we felt that connection. And from all the years I dated people, the one thing I want you to know is that when you know, you'll know. Don't settle. Go be you. Go be the real best you can be so that you will attract the real best of somebody else. They're out there! I promise you that so don't settle. Be the best you. Be real. Be honest. There will be struggles. But when it's right, it's right and you'll know it. So go be it. Be the radiant, radical and real you!

http://djjabin.com

Sorority Sisters –

If you were in a sorority, your old sorority sisters may be a great networking resource for you. They know you and will likely want to help you meet a great guy. Many may be married, and they and

39

their husbands may know available men. Even if they're single, they may know some quality guys who are not right for them, but may be perfect for you.

High School and College Friends –

You may sometimes wonder what happened to old high school and college boyfriends and other male friends you had from school. These days they can often be found on social networking platforms like Facebook, Twitter and LinkedIn. If these guys are unattached, they may be very happy to hear from you. Always attend high school and college reunions — see the discussion of reunions in Chapter 11.

Chapter 9
Men You Already Know

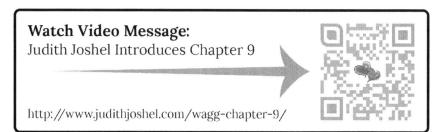

Watch Video Message:
Judith Joshel Introduces Chapter 9

http://www.judithjoshel.com/wagg-chapter-9/

You may be surprised to learn that many women marry men they already know — often someone they've known for a while, sometimes for many years. Many women to whom this has happened had never considered the guy they eventually married as a possible life partner. Maybe he was married or in a serious relationship with someone else, sometimes even with her girlfriend. Maybe he was single when she originally met him, but she was not. Even more interesting, she may initially have felt little or no chemistry with him. This may be shocking for many of you who have chosen men based solely or largely on chemistry. But, think about it — just because you have strong chemistry with a guy, doesn't mean that he has good character, that he wants a committed relationship, that you have much in common with him, or that he'll be able to make you happy.

These inspiring true stories will clarify my point. When my former client Brenda was in college, she had a tight group of friends, including Tony. Tony had a secret crush on her, but Brenda had a boyfriend and Tony had never told her how he felt about her. Fast forward 20 years. Brenda had been divorced for 4 years. She went to a college reunion and ran into Tony. They were delighted to see each other. Tony told Brenda that he was also divorced, and he confessed that he'd always had a crush on her and has fantasized about trying to find her over the years. He asked Brenda out, and she accepted. They started dating casually and found that they still had a lot in common and really enjoyed each other's company.

They took it slowly because they had both experienced painful divorces, and they understood the dangers of rushing too quickly into an exclusive relationship. After several months, however, they decided to make their relationship exclusive. They are now engaged to be married and couldn't be happier.

My friend and colleague Nijole Sparkis had known her husband Fritz for over 4 years before their relationship became romantic. They had a number of friends in common and would run into each other every 6 months or so at various events. But each was always in a relationship, and they didn't know each other well. At some point, Nijole became determined to win a trip to Egypt, which a local radio station was giving away as a promotion. She was studying spiritual principles and decided to apply what she was learning in order to win.

A singing teacher at the time, Nijole was amazed when one of her students won the Egypt trip instead. While she was thrilled for her student, she was also devastated because as much as she longed to visit Egypt, she couldn't begin to afford going on her own. It seemed as if the perfect storm of disappointment had just hit her head on. The best relationship she'd ever had had recently ended. She felt she'd never find anyone else, that she was too old now, that all the good men were taken.

She had previously made plans with her ex boyfriend to go to a concert, but sadly, there she was — with an extra ticket and no one with whom to go. In the meantime, Nijole had asked practitioners at the Agape Spiritual Center where she was studying to pray for her for 30 days. On the 30th day, the day before the concert, she ran into Fritz, who was also recently single, although Nijole didn't know that. On a whim, she offered him the extra ticket. He was delighted.

They attended the concert together, both believing that the other was romantically involved with someone else. Because of their assumptions, they felt no pressure and had an amazing time. By the end of the evening, they both knew they were soul mates. A week later Fritz phoned Nijole and told her he was going out of town for work. He then asked her to join him, inviting her to sing in a video shoot inside the Great Pyramid in Egypt for a proposed NBC Special. Nijole had waited a long time, but ultimately she not only got the trip to Egypt she'd dreamed about, but she also walked down the aisle with an awesome husband. They celebrated their 20th wedding anniversary in September of 2017.

My coaches Rachael Jayne and Datta Groover first met at Toastmaster meetings where they were practicing their public speaking skills. They liked each other, but neither felt romantic towards the other. Several years later, Rachael Jayne, who's a talented singer, was looking for a bass player for her band and someone suggested Datta. During rehearsals, they got to know each other better and eventually realized they were very well suited. Rachael Jayne had never had a long-term relationship and was becoming increasingly discouraged about finding her beloved. Datta, on the other hand, had been married three times and was determined that this time he was going to get it right. They've been married now for 9 years and are partners in a very successful coaching practice, which they've built together.

So be on the lookout for guys you know from the past. One of them may be a perfect match for you now. You're likely to have changed, and he also may have changed. Your life situations now may also be very different from when you had originally known each other. He might be in your current social sphere or he might not. You may unexpectedly run into him at an event or party or even on the street. The key is to be open. The guy who was not right for you 10 or 15 years ago may be absolutely right for you now. And he may want to connect with you just as much as you want to connect with him.

Watch Video Message from Veronica Strachan

http://www.judithjoshel.com/veronica-strachan/

Veronica is a writer, speaker, coach, facilitator and change specialist who is passionate about health and well-being, especially for rural communities. She works with remarkable women leaders who want to make a powerful and compassionate impact on the world. Her writing, programs, tools and strategies move women from "I can't" to "I can", so that they confidently show up, lead from the front, and inspire their teams to radically transform lives.

I met Ian in 1977 in high school chemistry class. We were both new to the school but he was not new to knowing about me. His best mate's mom had been my French and geography teacher, and he had been correcting my homework for some time. So he knew a little bit about me or at least how good I was or not in French and geography. So we became friends, hung out in a group and really didn't get together until a number of years later. Eventually we got married 8 years later in 1985 and we have been married for 32 years. What I love the most about Ian is that our love is unusual. It's more about witnessing – being there for the small wins and the day-to-day chores as well as for planning the big events and being there for the joyous events like the birth of our four children. It's also about being there for the tough times just as when our second daughter died just before she was 5. So bearing witness to each other's life and him loving me feisty, fabulous and flawed is very much a part of what our love is. My suggestion is don't settle for somebody who just sees the outside of you. Look for someone who looks past the superficial, someone you're prepared to spend a lifetime with and that you're prepared to be a witness in their life as well. Works for me.

http://www.veronicastrachan.com

Chapter 10
Men in Your Daily Life

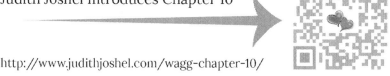

Watch Video Message:
Judith Joshel Introduces Chapter 10

http://www.judithjoshel.com/wagg-chapter-10/

Every day we cross paths with many people and some are single quality guys. We go about our lives with varying degrees of unconsciousness, doing our daily tasks in automatic mode and often not in tune with the people around us. This is where your **Man Radar** comes in. You'll want to get your eyes off your screen and get present in the moment. Being present means being completely aware of what's going on around you, including being aware of men who are nearby. Instead of accepting the belief that there are few if any quality single guys out there, try out this belief instead: "I'm excited to go about my life. I'm open to whatever comes my way. Awesome available men may be anywhere and everywhere I go." Use this as an affirmation as you go about your daily life. Practice this for 4 weeks and notice how you start observing many more men.

Think of all these venues as potential places to meet Mr. Right.

- **Public Transportation**. If you don't drive to and from work, you may ride on a bus, train or subway. So do guys. Stay alert for attractive men in these venues, smile and stand or sit near them. Any remark will serve as a conversation starter — even if it's about the weather or the heavy traffic that morning. It doesn't matter much what you say — if he's interested, he'll pick up the ball and carry the conversation forward. As you practice with your **Man Radar**, you may notice the same guys on a regular basis. And when you get used to seeing a guy, it will feel natural to smile and chat.

- **Carpools and Ride Shares**. Some metropolitan areas and some employers offer ways for commuters to join carpools and to connect with more casual ride shares. Cynthia, with whom I used to work, met her husband Brad on a ride share from Berkeley to their jobs in San Francisco. Most days, he drove into San Francisco, often stopping to pick up car poolers. She started riding with him several times a week and soon they discovered that they both were passionately interested in dancing. He asked her to go zydeco dancing with him one Friday night, and 10 years later they are happily married with a child, and they go out dancing together at least once a week.

- **Walking on the Street**. When I was single, I met several guys I ended up dating while I walking down the street. So be aware of who's walking nearby. If a guy is interested, he's likely to smile and say hello. If he gets a positive reaction from you, he may stop and chat, especially if you're warm and welcoming. My friend Chris met her husband while walking her dog in her neighborhood. And Rachel, a former client, is seriously dating a guy she met in the same way.

- **Coffee Shops**. These are great places to meet men. You can easily chat with guys near you in line. If you're sitting at a table, you can ask a guy sitting at the next table a question. Make eye contact and smile at an attractive guy walking by your table and he may ask if he might join you. Cindy, one of my clients, met her beloved husband while standing in line at Starbucks. It was just before Christmas, and she asked him if he'd ever had an eggnog latte. The rest is history.

- **Communal Tables**. Some restaurants, coffee shops and bakeries have communal tables. Always choose to sit at the communal table if there's room and be friendly and open to conversation.

- **On Your Lunch Break**. If you go to the same café or restaurant regularly, you'll start to notice other regulars. Smile and be friendly. If the weather's good, you may eat your lunch outside and there may be others around, including an interesting guy or two. By your body language, indicate that you're open to conversation and look for a chance to smile and to say something.

- **Grocery Store**. Single guys need to eat and will stop at the grocery store after work just like you. You'll most likely find them in the prepared and frozen food sections. So always check out these sections. A friendly smile and a question about a food item may start a conversation.

- **Laundromats**. If you don't have your own washer and dryer, you may do your own laundry. Single guys frequent laundromats, too. The best times to find them there are on weekends, especially Saturday mornings and later on Sunday. In bigger cities, there are **laundromat coffee houses** and **laundromat bars**. These are great bets for meeting single available guys. You have to do your laundry anyway, so why not go to a laundromat where you can have coffee or a beer and a chance to socialize?

Elena met her husband Jim in a laundromat. He had put way too much detergent in a washing machine and the soapsuds were seeping out of the washer onto the floor. Elena was amused, but she was also ready to lend a hand. She located an employee to help clean up the mess. Jim was embarrassed and amused at the same time and very grateful for Elena's help. He asked if he could take her to dinner at a nearby restaurant, and they both came away from the evening feeling good about each other. Jim, however, was involved in another relationship. When that relationship ended a few months later, he contacted Elena, who had also just ended a relationship. Neither was ready for anything serious, so things moved slowly for a while. Eventually, however, they moved into exclusive territory. They are now happily married and very busy with their little twin boys.

- **Dry Cleaners**. Single professional men who need to dress well frequent dry cleaners. If you also use dry cleaners, go before or after work or on a Saturday and be friendly to attractive male customers.

- **Jury Duty**. When I was in my 20s, I met a delightful guy, who later became my boyfriend, when I was on jury duty. He was one of the lawyers on the case, and after the case was over, he asked me out. Lawyers aren't allowed to have contact with jurors outside the courtroom while their case is being tried, but they can after the verdict is announced. This is exactly what happened in my case. Excuse the pun!

  While you're waiting to be called as a juror, you'll likely to be in a large waiting room with other jurors. When people are sitting around waiting, they are often open to conversation. If you see a guy who interests you, grab a seat near him. If you are chosen for a jury, you'll get an intense look at your fellow jurors during jury negotiations. Jurors often go out to lunch together and really get to know each other, sometimes better than people who have been dating for years. So don't try to get out of that jury summons. I know a happily married couple who met when they served as jurors on a criminal case.

- **Waiting Rooms** of all kinds are good places to strike up conversations with strangers. Be friendly to any attractive guys in the waiting rooms of your doctor, dentist, CPA, and car repair shop.

- The same goes for **Lines.** Whenever you find yourself waiting in line, remind yourself to be aware of others around you. Look for the chance to be friendly to any interesting man you see at the DMV, post office, Fed Ex store, copy shop, and bank. You're smart. You get the idea.

- **Gas Pump**. I've seen a number of guys start conversations with women at the next gas pump. If there's an attractive guy filling his tank near you, make eye contact and smile.

- **Common Areas in Your Apartment Building**. Many apartment buildings and condos have common areas like lobbies, elevators, halls, grounds, pools and fitness centers. These common areas give you a chance to check out and talk to other residents and their guests. When a guy's a neighbor and you see him around from time to time, it's easy to be friendly and strike up a conversation. You might even want to invite all your neighbors over for a pot-luck or for dessert one evening.

Chapter 11
Life Event Gatherings

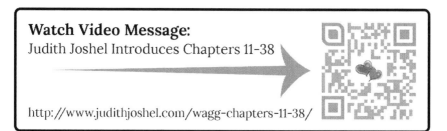

Watch Video Message:
Judith Joshel Introduces Chapters 11-38

http://www.judithjoshel.com/wagg-chapters-11-38/

Life event gatherings are especially good places to meet good single men. They are filled with people who are connected to each other in some way, and this usually makes them safe venues to meet unattached guys who know people you know. I am talking about:

- **Weddings**. My former client Laura met her husband at a wedding of mutual friends. He is a friend of the bride, and she is a relative of the groom. Weddings are romantic events celebrating love and commitment, so the energy is right for making a romantic connection. Never pass up a wedding invitation, even if you feel awkward going without a date.

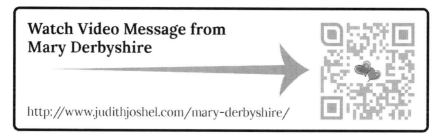

Watch Video Message from Mary Derbyshire

http://www.judithjoshel.com/mary-derbyshire/

Mary Derbyshire is a movement and fitness coach and Alexander Technique teacher. Her book, "Agility at Any Age: Discover the Secret to Balance, Mobility and Confidence" is an Amazon bestseller. Although Mary works with people of all ages, she is most passionate about getting Baby Boomers out of pain and moving with improved balance, mobility and ease.

I want to tell you how I met my husband. I first met him many years ago when we were in college very briefly. He was friends with my college roommate and then I never saw him again. Nine years after that auspicious day, I went to my college roommate's wedding and there he was. I met him again. He was tall and slender and very handsome and charming. He was very good friends with my college roommate and they lived across the street from each other. When I got to the wedding and met him, our mutual college friends started saying, "John and Mary would be perfect together – they'd be a perfect match." So they worked behind the scenes and got us together and got us dancing and talking and the sparks began to fly. He lived in Chicago and I lived in Boston and we had a long-distance courtship. I'd go to Chicago and he'd come to Boston. He was just starting a business and I was a starving artist so it's not like we could see each other every weekend. That was September when we started dating and by March he said, "Hey, let's get married. What do you think about getting married?" And I thought this is kind of fast, but why not? He actually went to my father first and did the old-fashioned thing – asked for my hand in marriage. Not that we're all that traditional, but it meant a lot to my parents. We were thinking about getting married a year and a half later. But my father said, "No, no, long-distance relationships are very difficult to keep." He and my mom had one. "Why don't you get married sooner rather than later?" So we got married in one year from the same weekend we met. We met on September 15th and got married on September 15th. Two days before our wedding, I sat down and tallied all the days we physically were together and in that one year including the 5 days before the wedding, we had been together for 28 days, which is pretty unbelievable. It was very scary when we tallied it up. We've been married for 27 years and we have 3 beautiful children and we've had a really wonderful, incredible relationship. He is sensitive and funny and smart and he listens really well. It's just been a really great adventure!

http://www.mderbyshire.com

- **Funerals**. Unless you or he are in deep mourning, it's even possible to meet a great guy at a funeral, a visitation or at a meal or open house after a funeral. Keep an open mind.

I met a middle-aged couple whose mothers had been best friends. This couple had also been friends from childhood, but both had married, and they each had moved away from their small town in Wisconsin and had lost contact. However, when his mother died, she came back for the funeral, as her mother was devastated about losing her best friend. The couple spent a few days together and realized that each was unhappy with their mates, but they were totally suited for one another. Each divorced their spouses. A year later, they were happily married and living in Chicago – where he is a judge.

- **Coed Wedding Showers, Baby Showers, Engagement Parties, and Anniversary Parties.** Many couples host coed wedding and baby showers as well as coed engagement and anniversary parties. Single male friends of the couple are likely to be there and there's usually time for socializing. Don't turn down these invitations!

- **Baptisms and Christenings**. Again single male relatives and friends of the family may attend.

- **Bar and Bat Mitzvahs** are happy affairs often attended by many guests. Go, eat, dance, have a great time, and keep your eyes open for attractive unattached guys.

- **High School and College Reunions**. Countless romances have started or have been rekindled at high school and college reunions. Some of your old classmates may be divorced, and there's nothing like a reunion to bring back the feelings from an adolescent crush. Sometimes couples who hardly knew each other in high school or college rediscover each other at a reunion. Many marriages have resulted between people reconnecting at reunions.

- **Family Reunions**. Attend family reunions, especially if the reunion is large. Hundreds of people attend some family reunions, and you never know who'll be there. You may meet a distant cousin or an aunt you haven't seen in years who just may know the perfect guy for you.

Chapter 12
Social Activities and Events

Social activities and events offer no-brainer opportunities to meet single guys and people who could introduce you to single guys.

- **Parties**. Accept invitations to parties. They can be great venues to meet single men. Be on the lookout for:

- **Birthday Parties** – for children as well as adults. You may not think a children's birthday party would be a good place to meet a single guy - but it absolutely can be. The child's parents may have invited their single male friends and relatives. And fathers of some of the child guests may be unattached.

- **New Years Eve and New Years Day Parties**. ~~Consider hosting a New Years Day party yourself. It's a great~~ way to start the new year.

- **Valentines Day Party.** How about hosting a **Valentines Day No Dates Allowed Party**? Require each woman you invite to bring a single man she's not romantically interested in, so all the women will get to meet new guys.

- **Other Types of Holiday Parties.** Holiday parties can be festive and fun, including:

    - **Halloween Costume Parties**
    - **St. Patrick's Day Parties**
    - **Tree Trimming Parties** and
    - **Christmas Caroling Parties.**

Don't be shy about organizing a holiday party yourself. Many singles ~~don't have anything to do~~ on holidays and would love an invitation. Ask one or two girlfriends it they'd like to organize it with you and you'll enjoy the preparation as well as the party.

- **Neighborhood Block Parties, Apartment Parties, Condo Parties**.

- **Oscar Watching Parties.** Consider hosting an Oscar Watching Party where your guests are invited to dress up like the stars. Or if that doesn't appeal to you, host the party, anyway, and give out ballots listing all the contenders. You can even place bets, and the one who wins the most categories, takes home the cash. Even if you don't win the contest, hopefully, you'll take top prize, making at least one good contact – and maybe even a potential relationship.

- **Holiday Picnics.** Many families host picnics on holidays like Memorial Day, July 4th and Labor Day. Consider organizing a holiday picnic with friends or contact the organizer of a singles Meetup Group and volunteer to help organize a holiday picnic for the group. [See the discussion about Meetup Groups in the next chapter.]

Chapter 13
Meetups, EventBrite and Yelp Events

- **Meetup Groups**. If you don't know where to start looking for Mr. Right, try **meetup groups**. Just google "meetup groups" and the name of your town or city. If you've never done this, get ready to be blown away by the number and variety of meetup groups you will find. No matter what your interests or the interests of the men you'd like to meet, you're likely to find a meetup group focused on that interest. The bigger your city, the more meetup groups you'll find. For example, in the San Francisco Bay Area, there are meetup groups for people who like to:

    Hike
    Bike
    Ski
    Read and discuss books
    Cook
    Write
    Drink beer
    Taste wine
    Dine out together
    Watch films
    Attend concerts
    Sketch
    Paint
    Play beach volleyball
    Attend cultural events
    Speak Spanish
    Play board games
    Run
    Speak Mandarin
    Meditate
    Have fun!
    Take photographs

Hike with their dogs
Listen to jazz and blues
Play pickup volleyball

There are meetup groups for single parents, Asian Americans and friends of Europe. There are also many meetup groups for people involved in or interested in technology, business and finance. Pay attention here because these groups tend to be filled with men.

These are just a fraction of the Bay Area meetup groups. There are many many meetup groups in almost all urban and suburban areas in the U.S., Canada, New Zealand, and western Europe. Many of them have thousands of members, including meetup groups for singles of different ages. These groups are filled with singles wanting to meet other singles in casual settings like hikes, dining out, and attending concerts. Groups are usually directed toward people of certain age ranges like 20s to 30s, over 40, over 50, and so on.

If you don't see a meetup group that fits your interest, start one. It's easy. Go to the meetup site to learn how. Alicia, one of my former clients, was feeling lonely for girlfriends. She had just moved to a new city for her job and had left a tight-knit group of girlfriends behind. We discussed her problem and she decided to start a girlfriend meetup group. It took about two months to get off the ground, but now it has several hundred members and sponsors an event every other week. Through it, Alicia has made two close girlfriends and a number of other more casual friends.

Alicia then met Todd, now her husband, on a cycling meetup ride. Coincidentally, Alicia and Todd had almost decided not to go on that ride. Alicia was feeling very stressed out from work, and Todd was just recovering from a cold. At the last minute, they each decided to choose a ride that was much easier than the rides they usually took. They've been together ever since.

My lovely client Deborah asked me to share her meetup group experience with you.

"One Saturday night I'd had enough. Sitting at home on my own on a Saturday night is just not good for me. A meetup group had a night planned at a live music venue and an artist I really like was playing. In two minutes I was on my way. I joined the few girls who were there and danced. We all had a great time.

"At the end of the evening, one of the girls asked if she could give my number to her friend who was the leader of the group. I casually said. 'Sure he can call me or I'll see him at the next event. I didn't think she would actually give him my number or if she did, I didn't think he would ring. I was wrong. He called the next day, and two days later we went out on our first date. Time will tell if we are right for each other. *Even meeting through meetup groups*

"We've discussed when and how meetup groups should be a part of our lives. He leads his own group and I lead my own group. We have gone together to each other's group. I really think meetup groups are great. They provide ways to explore your interests and meet others with similar interests. Meetup groups also give you a way to get out of the house. You don't have to stop attending the meetup when you find a relationship."

- **Eventbrite Events**. Eventbrite sponsors activities and events, which you'll want to check out on a regular basis. Google "Eventbrite" and the name of your city. Many different kinds of events appear on the Eventbrite site from expensive trainings of one sort or another to free community events. You never know what you're going to discover there. You might find a charity event, a food festival, an International Pillow Fight Day activity, a dance concert, and so on.

- **Yelp Events**. Yelp sponsors events from fairs and festivals to dog trainings. A few will be specifically for singles while others will attract some singles. Google "Yelp events" and the name of your city to find them. My colleague Nicole met her beloved husband Gabriel at a Yelp-sponsored Halloween party.

Chapter 14
Singles Events and Activities

Many singles shy away from singles events and activities. As I stated in an earlier chapter, if that includes you – again I want to challenge you to rethink that stance. When I was single, I often avoided these events and activities because I felt a lot of pressure when I actually went to them. Sometimes there weren't many men, and I rarely found the men who did attend that attractive. But many of my clients have met terrific guys at singles events, and sometimes I did too. So before you reject meeting guys this way, try several different kinds of activities and venues. I would start with **Speed Dating**.

- **Speed Dating** is fun, really fun. You get to meet 8-15 or even 20 guys in your age range, talking to each one for 3-7 minutes as they move around the circle or down the line to sit opposite you. Afterwards there is usually time to have a drink and socialize.

The most frequent objections I hear from women about speed dating are: "It's so superficial. You just get to talk to guys for a few minutes and then you both decide if you want to exchange contact information. That isn't enough time." Absolutely it's superficial, but so are many first conversations with new guys. It is, however, long enough to get a feel for a guy to see if you'd like to spend more time talking with him.

Deciding whether or not to meet a guy based on his online profile could be considered just as superficial, but people do it all the time and many marriages are the result of online dating. When you meet guys offline, your initial conversation may be quite superficial, but that really doesn't matter. Your goal should be just trying to get a feel for him and whether you'd like to spend a little more time getting to know him better. You aren't trying to determine if he's the one. In fact, you will have no idea if he's the one no matter how attracted you may be to him. It takes time to determine that. So, don't dismiss speed dating as superficial.

If you're very shy, the thought of making small talk for 5 minutes with 10 guys may terrify you. Or you may be coming out of a divorce and feeling overwhelmed with the whole dating scene. Promise yourself some small reward and go anyway. Tell yourself to concentrate on looking feminine and feeling your best - and on being warm and inviting. You don't have to say anything brilliant. If you're really shy, sit back, make eye contact with the guy and smile warmly. If you don't know what to say, let him lead. Just listen and respond. Be curious about whatever he says. Be prepared with a few questions in case he's really shy too. For example, you could ask him, "What's the funniest movie you've ever seen?" Or "Where do you most want to go on your next vacation?" Or "If you could have anything in the world, what would that be?"

If you'll attend 2-3 speed-dating events, you'll find yourself feeling more comfortable around single men, and this will serve you brilliantly in your dating life. It doesn't matter if no guys choose you for further contact or if you have no interest in further contact with any of them. What matters is that you have had the courage to put yourself in a situation which felt uncomfortable, and you gave yourself the chance to practice smiling, flirting and briefly talking to a number of guys. Always keep in mind why you're practicing: You want to be ready to meet your Mr. Right when he comes along.

The first time I tried speed dating, no one I was interested in showed interest in me. But the experience helped me feel more confident about making small talk with lots of guys – and I went again. The second time I met two men whom I dated for a while. Neither turned out to be my Mr. Right, but they were both great guys, just not the right matches for me after I got to know them.

Two of my clients in their 50s are dating quality men they met at speed dating events. Will they end up with these guys? It's too soon to tell, but they would certainly encourage you to give speed dating a try.

My former client Lisa met her husband Chris at a speed-dating event. He was really taken with her. She thought he was handsome, but he seemed too smooth, not her type at all. She did, however, agree to meet for a short coffee date after the event and they got wrapped up in an intense conversation. After three hours, they still had tons more to say to each other. That was the start of their two-year romance, which resulted in marriage and two adorable kids.

- **Singles Activity Groups.** There are thousands of singles groups geared to various age ranges and types of activities. Believe it or not, there are over 10,000 singles meetup groups worldwide! Some are focused on singles in their 20s and 30s, some on singles over 30, over 40, and over 50. Some are focused on dining out, others on hiking and other outdoor activities. There will also be singles like you in many meetup groups which aren't specifically for singles. See Chapter 13 above for more on meetups. Some of the singles meetup groups are:

  - 60+ active singles
  - Single professionals
  - Single parents
  - Black singles
  - Cycling singles
  - 30s and 40s fun activities
  - Christian singles
  - Spiritual singles

Try the singles groups that may be a fit for you. Even if you don't meet anyone the first time, be willing to give the meetup another try or two. You may have hit the group on an off day and your Mr. Right may be at the next meetup activity.

- **Match.com In Person Stir Events.** Even though you don't want to participate in online dating, consider signing up for **Match.com** to get access to their in person stir events. Match holds these events in almost all metropolitan areas. They are mostly happy hours, but they sponsor other kinds of events as well such as dance lessons and game nights.

Chapter 15
Work-Related Ways to Meet Men

In Chapter 8 on Networking I discuss meeting men at work and through people you know through work. Here are some other work-related ways to meet single guys.

- **Business Conferences and Conventions and Industry Meetings** can be great places to meet single men working in your field or a related field. There are often happy hours and other opportunities to socialize at conferences, conventions and meetings. ⌐ ⸙B Pages .

- **Professional Groups.** Attend **Young Professionals** meetings and join professional groups in your field like **bar and medical associations.** Attend meetings and other functions hosted by these groups with an eye toward meeting guys as well as nurturing your professional education and relationships.

- **Corporate Sponsored Events.** Your corporate employer may sponsor golf outings, volleyball tournaments and other events and activities. These events give you a chance to meet men outside your particular department and area of expertise.

- **Employer Holiday Parties** provide opportunities to socialize with co-workers. You'll want to limit your alcohol intake and be clear that you are not open to romantic involvement with anyone you work with or may be working with in the future – especially not with anyone who is or may become your supervisor or someone you supervise. Many people have gotten themselves into difficult situations at the annual holiday party. You don't want to be one of them.

- **Part-time Jobs in Businesses Frequented by Men**. If you're in the market for a part-time job, look for jobs in businesses where you'll come in contact with lots of men. Places to consider are gyms and fitness clubs, men's clothing stores, stores selling computers, phones and other techie items, and restaurants frequented by men.

- **Business Networking Organizations.** There are a number of organizations catering to business people, but you don't have to be a business person to become a member of many of them. Here are some possibilities:

- **Chamber of Commerce.** If you're an entrepreneur, check out your local **Chamber of Commerce.** These organizations sponsor regular meetings where you can meet other entrepreneurs and learn about topics that may be of interest to you. You can network there to build your business and to socialize with single male members – a great use of your time .

- **Toastmasters Clubs** have many business-oriented members who want to develop their public speaking skills in a supportive atmosphere. These are great venues meet new people. My coaches Rachael Jayne and Datta Groover initially met at Toastmasters meetings, and then got romantically involved years later. Their story is in Chapter 9.

- **Rotary Clubs** attract professional and business people who want to be of service in their communities. You'll find lots of generous-minded people in these clubs.

- **BNI or Business Networking International** is a business networking and referral organization that has chapters all over the U.S. and in many other countries. It's a great way to grow your business and to meet other business people. I was once a member and found the other members friendly and very helpful. Although the main purpose of joining BNI is to promote your business, the organization is also a potential place to meet single male business owners. I know of a chiropractor who met her attorney husband in her local BNI chapter. They've been married for 11 years and have 2 great kids.

- **Anti-Cafes**. If you're self-employed and live in or near a large city, check out **Anti-Cafes.** Anti-Cafes, appearing in a number of cities now, will give you a quieter, less crowded place to work than your local Starbucks. You'll be surrounded by other self-employed people also working away on their laptops. As an added benefit, your shared workspace will give you access to coffee and goodies. Some Anti-Cafes charge a flat reasonable monthly fee. Others charge by the hour. What better place could there be to meet single self-employed guys in a casual way? And some Anti-Cafes even have daily social happy hours.

Chapter 16
Guys Who Love Sports

Not all guys love sports, but gazillions do. Whether you are participating with them or watching a game next to them, you a have wonderful opportunity to meet them on their own turf.

Participating in sports is a powerful way to meet guys. I recommend it to every woman who's single and looking, unless she can't participate due to a disability or absolutely hates the sport. But even if you do hate participating in sports, I challenge you to find one you might enjoy. It doesn't have to be vigorous. Why not give golf or swimming or boating a try?

And if you're not young and are wondering what on earth I'm suggesting, as this seems totally unrealistic – Laura's story may change your mind. My good friend Laura is 70 and has been divorced for years. She became concerned about her weight, so a year or two ago, she started going to a kick boxing class to help her lose the extra pounds and get more physically fit. Guess what. She met Matthew in that class. He's four years younger and completely nuts about her. Though the participants in the class were almost all women, Laura was warm and welcoming to Matthew and a few months ago, he started pursuing her. They're now an item and couldn't be happier. They just returned from a trip to Europe and are already planning their next adventure. (And as an added incentive, many people have found kickboxing to be a very effective anti-depressant.)

Consider Participating in These Sports:

- **Running**. Lots of guys run for fitness, competition and fun in all sorts of venues. If you're just starting to run, consider running short distances at a local track or park. My girlfriends Susan and Lynn used to run. They both met a number of guys when they ran at a nearby track and through their neighborhoods. If you like to run, consider joining a local running club.

Some of the guys will be serious runners, and others will be into it for fitness and fun. There are all sorts of venues for running and races. Watch for charity races, fun runs, and marathons. My cousin met her husband in a running club where she was preparing for a marathon. She had never run in her life, but when she started running, she found she loved it. Her totally unexpected bonus was meeting Mike, another marathon runner who eventually became her terrific husband.

- **Golf**. Golf is very popular with men, especially with successful professionals and businessmen, but men from all walks of life love it. It's a social game that's usually played with others. You have lots of time to talk with your fellow players while you're getting outdoor exercise usually on a lovely course. Often you can find a **lounge, a bar and/or a restaurant at the clubhouse** and a **golf shop**, all of which present further opportunities for socializing. I recommend golf to many of my clients. If you don't know how to play, invest in some lessons and see how you like it. Also frequent your local **Driving Ranges** to work on your swing. Choose a spot next to an attractive guy and ask for his feedback. A good guy will love to share some tips with you. Who knows where this might lead if he's unattached? Play on a **Chip and Putt Course** or on a **Miniature Golf Course** to practice your putting. There just might be an attractive man doing the same thing.

If you enjoy golf and if you can afford it, check out your nearby **Country Clubs** and consider joining one. There will be lots of opportunities to meet fellow Country Club members at various club functions. And you'll always be welcome in the club lounge and restaurant. Here's another great tip. Check out whether the **American Singles Golf Association** has any events in your area at **singlesgolf.com**. This is a great way to meet single male golfers.

- **Skiing**. Skiing is a terrific way to meet men – both **Downhill and Cross Country Sking**. Ski slopes, ski lifts, cross-country ski trails, warming huts, and lodges are full of them, as are ski resorts and lodges. If you want a break from skiing, hang around the ski lodge fireplace with a hot drink. Be open and friendly. Look into joining a local **Ski Club** that sponsors trips to the slopes. You may meet quality single guys at club meetings and also on the ski bus to the slopes. Try to sit beside an attractive guy on the bus. And note: there are often ski clubs for singles. Also consider trying out **Snowshoeing.** It's an activity that attracts many men.

- **Rock Climbing** If you're athletic and adventurous, consider rock climbing. You'll find indoor rock climbing gyms in many cities, and most offer lessons for beginners. Sign up for lessons and go often to practice. This activity attracts many many men. While better climbers may not want a beginner for a partner, other climbers will, and many will be very happy to share some pointers if you ask for their help. Some rock climbing gyms also offer have social activities for their members – an extra bonus.

- **Biking**. Biking attracts large numbers of men. Check out **bike clubs** in your area. Some may be meetup groups. If you have a bike and aren't in good shape, go on some easy rides and build up your stamina. If you don't have a bike, try renting or borrowing one to see if you like it. There will likely be some men on the easy rides, but many will be more advanced riders as well as racers. Most bike clubs sponsor regular group rides of varying difficulty. Many also sponsor or participate in long rides and races like the century, a 100 mile race. Even if you're not in shape for the complete race, you could bike for part of it and then volunteer in a support role and go out for a meal with your fellow bikers after the race.

There are also a number of long rides lasting from a couple days to a month or more that are **fundraisers for causes like cancer and Aids.** These rides attract guys who love to bike and want to contribute to a good cause. Lots of them are likely to be high quality and available. And don't forget **Spinning Classes** at your local Y, gym or fitness center; many men attend these classes. **REI stores** and **bike shops** may offer **classes in how to ride, road biking, mountain biking and bike maintenance**. Check out **bike expos and bike festivals**. I know two women who met their husbands at the bike festival in Charlotte, North Carolina.

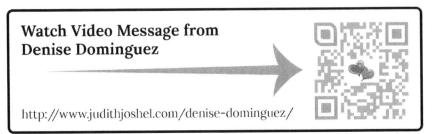

Watch Video Message from
Denise Dominguez

http://www.judithjoshel.com/denise-dominguez/

Denise Dominguez is a Woman's Empowerment Coach, International Best-Selling Author, and Speaker. Denise empowers women globally by having them face their fears and limiting beliefs that hinder them from living the life they dream of. Denise has a clear vision for seeing the trouble-spots that exist in every "stuck" situation and the creativity to transform it instantly.

I'm sharing with you today how I met my fiancée, Ray. It was 2013 and it was at Bikefest in downtown Raleigh. I looked over to see this guy like totally checking me out, staring me down. Whatever. I didn't think anything of it actually. There was a bunch of guys there, we were at a Bikefest and we were in front of a band playing in the street – the street was blocked off for the band to play. I went into a bar to use the bathroom. When I came out of the bathroom, there he was sitting there waiting for me and he struck up a conversation. His first line was, "Are ya single?" in his Boston accent and of course I started cracking up. To make a long story short, we were with some friends and we decided, all four of us, to go out and explore and we got separated so I didn't see him for the rest of the day. But I did remember his name and what city he was in so thankfully

when I put his name and city into Facebook bam he came up.
So we started connecting ~~then and we were friends for quite a~~
~~while before we started seeing each other~~ — it was over a year
and we started living together two years later from that time.
~~So that's how I met my~~ fiancée Ray in downtown Raleigh at
Bikefest. Yes you can find a guy off line and successfully.

http://www.denisedominguez.com/

- **Martial Arts. Learning** a martial art involves physical and mental training. Knowing that you are proficient in a martial art will give you increased confidence in all parts of your life. Martial Arts classes attract loads of men. Check out what's offered in your area, including Karate, Judo, Jujitsu, Tae Bo, Akido, and Taikwondo. See if you can do a trial class. This will give you a chance to see who the other students are and whether you think you'd like it before you sign up.

- **Sailing.** Lots of guys are into boating. If you live around water, explore **sailing lessons.** Ask around about where you can go in order to score an invitation to **crew on a sailboat.** Then go there. In areas where sailing is popular, **Sailing Clubs** will offer lessons, opportunities to crew, and social activities. Check them out. [Safety Tip: Don't go out on a boat with a guy you barely know unless others you do know are present; you're very vulnerable when you're on the water.]

- **Other Types of Boating.** Many guys are also into **yachting, canoeing, kyaking,** and **river rafting.** A number of organizations and businesses offer canoeing, kyaking and river rafting trips for groups. These activities attract physically fit single guys. And are also loads of fun.

- **Other Water-Related Sports.** Consider learning how to **Surf** or **Wind Surf. Snorkeling** and **Deep Sea Diving** attract lots of men. You can often get certification in deep sea diving at your local YMCA. Check out **Surf Shops** and **Diving Shops.** My cousin met her beloved when she visited his diving shop.

Watch Video Message from Beks Thompson

http://www.judithjoshel.com/beks-thompson/

Beks Thompson is an inspirational speaker, musician and creator of BE A BEACON transformational programmes for women. She has carved out a place for herself in the field of quality holistic health with over 20 years of experience in the allied health sector as a Physio, Yoga Teacher and Art of Feminine Presence Teacher. Beks is passionate about sharing practical embodied tools empowering women to shine a light for themselves and others to follow – without the burnout!

I'm Beks Thompson and I'd like to share a little about my relationship which has now spanned over 25 years with my partner Rich. We first met at uni at a diving club and he was one of my instructors. We weren't romantically drawn together to start with. We developed a friendship. I remember my friends and myself saying, "He's such a lovely guy but I just don't fancy him." But here we are almost 25 years later, we've been married for almost 11 years, we have two boys ages 11 and 13 and a half and we've also immigrated from England here to Australia. We've covered a lot of ground in those 25 years and it's not all been easy. I'd like to share a couple things that might help you on your journey toward a relationship or maybe in deepening your relationship. We have fundamental core beliefs that are very much the same around how we want to live our life, not necessarily around religion or spirituality, not even on the commitment we have around the sustainability of the environment. But deep down we have the real core fundamental ways that we see things that are similar. However, we are very different. He's very much the rock, happy to have a lot of still-

74

ness in his life, happy to just have connection with the family whereas I am a lot more dynamic, a lot more creative, probably a lot more emotional, but we find those things really balance us out. But initially and certainly in a long term relationship, they can also create some triggers and irritations within the relationship if you're not committed to that long term sustainability and growth. Over the long term it's so important that you spend time really deeply connecting on a profound deep level. We've done some work together on that because reactions and resentments build up over time and you need to be able to honor your differences as well as the things that are the same through having that commitment to having gratitude for all those things you originally saw and love about that person. Keeping that going throughout the relationship is invaluable as well as learning how to communicate your truth. I can truthfully say that after 25 years our relationship is the best that it has ever been.

www.beksthompson.com
www.facebook.com/zenphysiyoga
www.facebook.com/beks.thompson

- **Rowing Clubs**. In areas with rivers and lakes, there are often **coed rowing clubs**. Rowing is incredible exercise; lots of good guys are into it. Why not join a club where you'll see these guys regularly and get to know them in a non-pressured way?

- **Swimming Clubs.** If you enjoy swimming and are near any natural bodies of water, see if there are any adult swimming clubs. An example is the Dolphin Club in San Francisco. Members swim the San Francisco Bay and other nearby venues. They also row, and participate in triathlons.

- **Water Aerobics.** Water aerobics classes are a great way to stay in shape. Although many more women than men take these classes, a few men do participate.

- **Coed Sport Leagues**. Do you like to play softball, soccer or volleyball? There are coed softball, soccer and volleyball teams in many places. The games offer you a great chance to meet guys in a very natural way while you're having fun.

- **Fishing.** Many unattached fishermen would be delighted to meet a woman who enjoys fishing. If you live the Eastern U.S., check out the **LL Bean Outdoor Schools** for **fishing classes**. Classes are inexpensive or free. My client Jean has always wanted to learn to fly fish, so she signed up for a free **fly-fishing class** with **Orvis.** Since many men love **deep sea fishing,** if you have the chance, sign up for a class.

- **Sky Diving** and **Hang Gliding**. If you like risk and are looking for a guy who likes risk, consider sky-diving and hang gliding. You're likely to meet a number of adventurous men. But the risks from these sports are very real, so be sure you find a qualified, experienced teacher.

- **Squash, Handball, Raquetball, and Fencing.** These sports are loaded with men but few women. If you participate, you're sure meet lots of guys.

- **Bowling.** Many bowling alleys these days are updated and trendy. Some even have bars and cafes. There are **bowling leagues** in most cities and smaller towns. If you think you might be interested in joining, be a spectator first and see if there are any interesting guys participating before you join.

- **Tennis** attracts lots of guys. Take some lessons and go to courts in neighborhoods where the kinds of guys you'd like to meet may play. Practice against the wall and ask an attractive guy for advice on your swing. If you return to the same courts, you'll meet the regulars and are likely to get invitations to play with various people and to join them afterwards for food and/or drinks. My friend Pat met several boyfriends this way.

- **Tennis Clubs** attract tennis lovers who have some money, and they offer you the chance to socialize with other members. If you like tennis, check out your local tennis club.

- **Darts, Ping Pong** and **Pool**. Many men enjoy playing these sports. You can find these venues by Googling "playing darts" or "ping pong" or "playing pool" and the name of your city. There are bars where these sports are played. Look for recommendations on YELP. There are also **Ping Pong or table tennis clubs**, especially in areas with a Chinese population. **High-end pool halls** tend to attract wealthier guys.

- **Obstacle Course** fitness events attract many younger men. These venues include foot races with lots of obstacles like mud, walls to climb, and weights to carry. Many cities host obstacle course events. Participate if the spirit moves you. If not, why not go and watch? It's likely to be a lot of fun, and you'll be surrounded by competitive adventurous guys.

- **Orienteering** is an international competitive, challenging sport, a race that calls on your speed, your endurance and your brain. Participants use a map and a compass to navigate an unfamiliar terrain in a timed race. People of all ages participate at different difficulty levels, but generally you'll find increasing numbers of men at the higher levels of difficulty. Beginners are welcome, so if orienteering sounds interesting to you, check it out.

- **Sporting Goods and Equipment Stores**. Men frequent these stores. Check out general sporting goods stores and REI as well as more specialized stores for different sports like running, biking, surfing and diving shops. Two happily married couples I know met in sporting goods stores.

Watching Sports

Single guys from all walks of life love to watch sports. If you show an interest, many of them would love to watch sports with you. There are thousands of venues to meet guys who are sports fans. Some suggestions are:

- **Sports-Watching Parties**. Accept invitations to sports-watching parties like these:

  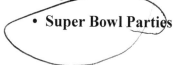
  - **Super Bowl Parties**

- **Kentucky Derby Parties**
- **Rose Bowl Parties**
- **World Series Parties**
- **Tailgate Parties**
- **Indianapolis 500 Parties**

Earlier, I had suggested hosting an Oscar party or a Valentine's Day party. If that's not your thing, consider **hosting your own sporting event party**. Ask each woman you invite to bring along an unattached guy in whom she isn't romantically interested. This is her price of admission.

- **Games**. Keep your eye open for attractive guys at:
  - **Football Games**
  - **Baseball Games**
  - **Soccer Games**
  - **Hockey Games**
  - **Basketball Games**

  Consider attending **college and professional games** as well as **major and minor league baseball games**. Sit near an attractive man if you can. Just smile and ask him a question about a play, a player or anything else related to the game. In all probability, unless he has a kid playing in the game, he's probably passionate about it or he wouldn't be there. Most good guys love to be helpful. You can also start conversations with guys standing in line at the refreshment counter.

- **Sports Bars** are totally worth frequenting to watch Monday Night Football, Sunday football games, the World Series, and any other big games. There are higher and lower end Sports Bars, so choose one where guys you'd like to meet are likely to go. If you're not a big sports fan, read up a little on the teams and the games before you go. This will help you ask knowledgeable questions – but don't worry if your questions are naive. If a guy finds you attractive, he'll be happy to talk with you about anything.

- **Nascar and Horse Races**. These can be lots of fun. Just be aware that gamblers are attracted to races and gamblers don't usually make great husbands. But good guys who don't have gambling problems also love racing, and lots of them will be at Nascar and horse races.

- **Polo Matches** are usually high-class affairs. Although polo is often played in clubs, club membership isn't usually required to attend matches. These are not blue jeans friendly venue, however. Casual smart to elegant dress is the norm. If you're looking to meet classier guys, check out polo matches if there are any in your area. If you're into polo for the love of the sport – and the possibility of meeting a man who may not be a club member, some cities, such Pacific Palisades, California, have polo matches once a week during the season. You can dress in jeans or whatever you'd like to attend these matches held in accessible lovely places, open to the public. In the Palisades, you can take a picnic, spread a blanket and eat on grounds across from the polo field. And who knows – you might find a friendly group also enjoying a picnic nearby.

- **Regattas.** A regatta is a series of boat races. Yacht races, sailboat races, rowing races and even motorboat races may be included. This is a great venue to meet guys who own and/or love boats and boat racing.

- **Supermarket Snack Aisle**. Visit the supermarket snack aisle and the **beer and soft drinks aisle** on a Football Sunday before the game. Single guys may be there stocking up for the game. Ask one of them which team he thinks is going to win. Unless he's in a terrible hurry or a bad mood, that question will definitely engage him.

Chapter 17
Guys Who Love Nature and the Outdoors

Guys who are involved in many of the sports discussed in the last chapter, including skiing, surfing, boating, biking and fishing, are probably passionate about spending time in the outdoors. You will also find guys who love being outdoors in nature participating in the following activities.

- **Hiking**. You can find hiking groups and men who enjoy hiking everywhere. There are countless meetup groups, Sierra Club groups and other local groups which sponsor hikes. Google "hiking groups" and the name of your city or town. There tend to be more men on the more difficult hikes so if you're a beginner or out of shape, start with easier hikes and build up.

- **Backpacking**. Backpacking is a wonderful way to get completely away from your regular life and out into remote natural areas. You can find backpacking groups in the same way you find hiking groups: google "backpacking groups" and the name of your city or town. Some of these groups offer backpacking training for beginners. But remember — backpacking is hard work and you need to be in good physical shape. Brenda, a lovely woman I know, met Brian, the man she married, on a backpacking trip sponsored by her college alumnae association. They've backpacked each summer for many years with their 3 children and are now introducing their grandchildren to the joys of back country adventures. For safety's sake, you'll want to check out any backpacking group and be sure you feel safe and comfortable with the members before backpacking into the wilderness with them.

- **Camping**. Camping is, of course, part of backpacking. But you don't have to carry a 40-pound pack into the wilderness to experience the joys of camping. There are meetup camping groups all over the world. You can drive to most of the campsites and carry your gear in your vehicle. The same backpacking safety warning applies to camping groups as well.

- **Birdwatching.** Birdwatching is a big deal. There are bird-watching groups everywhere. Some go on long hikes to remote areas, while others look for birds in urban areas. Some quality single men are very serious birdwatchers. If birds are your thing and you're interested in meeting people passionate about them, definitely check out your local birdwatching groups. Some are meetup groups and some are sponsored by the Audubon Society and other bird conservation organizations.

Chapter 18
Food and Drink Venues

You'll find single guys in many different types of restaurants, so keep your eyes open whenever you go out to eat. If there's an attractive guy sitting near you, catch his eye, smile and ask him a question about the food. Has he ever tried the lasagna? What on the menu does he recommend? Remember guys love to be helpful to women, so he'll probably be pleased if he can answer your question.

Men are likely to be in these kinds of **restaurant venues**:

- **Breakfast and Lunch Places in Financial and Business Districts.** If your schedule permits, check out breakfast places early on weekday mornings. If you find one with lots of male customers, return to it regularly. It becomes more comfortable to strike up a conversation with someone you've seen several times in the same venue. Also try **breakfast places in neighborhoods where lots of single men live**. That may be in your neighborhood OR in nearby neighborhoods.

- **Anti-Cafes.** I discussed Anti-Cafes in Chapter 15 but want to mention them again here. If you're self-employed, you may bring your laptop to your local Starbucks, but the noise and crowdedness can be distracting. As an antidote to Starbucks and other coffee shops, **Anti-Cafes** are starting to spring up in larger cities to give folks a communal, but quieter place to work along with access to coffee and food. They are often coffee shops housed in higher end restaurants that previously served only dinner, but sometimes **Anti-Cafes** have their own venues. Usually for a flat reasonable monthly fee, they provide a comfortable shared work space as well as unlimited coffee, tea and some food items. Some charge by the hour, so you can just drop in as the spirit moves you without having to commit to a monthly fee. If you work for yourself and live in or near a large city, see if any Anti-Cafes exist in your area. They are great places to meet self-employed single guys. Some Anti-Cafes have social happy hours later in the day giving you a natural way to meet that cute guy you've been eyeing across the room.

- **Coffee Shops and Bagel Shops.** Coffee shops and bagel shops can be great places to meet guys, particularly in the early morning, but also throughout the day. I met lots of single guys in coffee shops when I was single. If your eyes are not glued to your phone and you're present in the moment and ready to give a welcoming smile, you are giving guys an opening to approach you.

- **Donut Shops.** It's not just guys with unhealthy eating habits who frequent Donut Shops. Sometimes even healthy and fit guys indulge in this guilty pleasure. If a guy who indulges in donuts isn't a deal breaker for you, check out your local donut shop early in the morning.

- **Casual Restaurants with Dining Counters**. Sit at the counter. And of course, sit in an open seat next to an interesting-looking man. It may feel more comfortable starting a side-by-side conversation with a stranger than with someone sitting opposite you.

- **Sushi Bars.** The same thing goes for sushi bars where you're sitting side by side. My client Cathy met the love of her life during a crowded lunch hour at a Japanese restaurant. She wanted a small table of her own, but there was a 20-minute wait. As her schedule was tight, she decided to sit at the only open seat at the sushi bar — beside her future husband, Brian. They started talking about the sushi, and the conversation went from there to discussing their favorite restaurants. Discovering they were both serious foodies, Brian asked Cathy to join him for a meal at a new Thai restaurant she had never tried. They soon discovered that they were both passionate talented cooks, as well as foodies, and started cooking theme meals for themselves and their friends. The food at their wedding became an instant legend their friends and relatives still discuss. Cathy and Brian have been happily married for 5 years and have a beautiful 2-year-old son.

- **High End Restaurants.** Many higher end restaurants have **bars and lounge areas** which can be great places to meet men. You can order a drink at the bar and often a bite to eat, too. Be sure you're looking and feeling your most magnetic and try stopping in for a drink (non alcoholic is the best choice when you're looking to meet men) and maybe some food. Although lower end bars tend not to be the best places to meet quality men, higher end venues are. You don't have to stay for dinner. Stay for a little while and be friendly and open to conversation. Certain kinds of higher end restaurants like **Steak Houses** and **Restaurants at Marinas** tend to attract lots of men.

- **Food Festivals.** Food Festivals are fun and casual and many guys enjoy them. What's not to like if you love to eat? You have an obvious topic of conversation – the food – and who doesn't enjoy talking about the food they're tasting?

- **Food Trucks.** These days there are Food Trucks in many locations; many sell terrific food at reasonable prices. Be open to chatting with guys near you in line and see if there's an interesting looking guy to sit near while you're eating. Remember to challenge yourself to chat with the people near you whenever you're waiting in any kind of line.

- **Food Courts.** You have a choice of where to sit in a Food Court. If you see an attractive guy with an empty seat at his table, ask if you might join him.

- **Takeout Food Lines.** It's easy to strike up a conversation when you're both waiting in line at a **Deli**, the **Whole Foods takeout section**, and at **Fast Food Restaurants**.

- **Restaurants with Communal Tables.** These venues are ideal for meeting other singles. If you have the choice between a private and a communal table, choose the communal table.

- **Alcohol Venues.** Many couples with great marriages have met over a drink. My nephew, who is a real catch, met his awesome wife in a high-end bar. You can absolutely meet a great guy in these venues. But certain dangers come along with alcohol use, and I invite you to think through these dangers.

Even one alcoholic drink can impair your judgment and impulse control even if you have no problems with alcohol use. I have nothing against drinking in moderation, but for my clients and for you too, I recommend that you drink no alcohol when you are out trying to meet men and on early dates as well. I want you always to have 100% of your wits about you. Usually you know nothing about a man you've just met except what he may tell you. He may not be a good guy, and he may not be safe to be around. When you've had even one drink, your ability to notice any little red flags he may reveal and to take them seriously may be somewhat impaired, although you may feel completely normal.

I know, I know – some of you are protesting that it's completely unrealistic for me to recommend no alcohol in venues where everyone is drinking and is expected to do so. It will make you feel and seem totally out of it. It's hard enough to meet guys and this may make it impossible. If you were my client, I would ask you to examine your assumption about your need to drink while meeting guys and on early dates. Where does it come from and what does it mean in terms of the types of guys you want to meet? Since you're not my client, I am going to give you a pass to drink one and only one alcoholic drink during the course of an evening. You should also be eating some food and drinking water and other non-alcoholic drinks. That's it – one drink. No one can call you a teetotaler and if you also consume food and non-alcoholic beverages, you should be able to stay present and in control of yourself and your judgment.

Another bit of advice: When you meet a guy having a drink, note whether he may have a problem with alcohol. Alcoholism is very widespread, and if he's downing more than a couple drinks while you're observing him, he may have an alcohol problem. He may not, but his drinking behavior should be a red flag for you to take careful note of. And if you see him again – accidentally, or by choice - stay very aware of his drinking behavior. Ask yourself whether he's drinking too much and/or too often and whether you're seeing signs of inebriation like slurred speech. If you've had a parent who was or is an alcoholic or addict, you may be particularly drawn to men with alcohol problems.

I have worked with many women who have had alcoholic husbands and boyfriends, and I can assure you of what you probably already know: that your life will be deeply unhappy if you become seriously involved with a man with alcohol problems. One of my clients started working with me when she started seeing signs of alcohol abuse in her fiancé. Two of her former boyfriends had also shown signs of alcohol abuse, and her father had been alcoholic when she was growing up. Although my client and her fiance clearly loved each other, she decided to end the relationship after she confronted him with her concerns and he didn't take them seriously. As you can imagine, this decision was very painful for her, but it was much less painful than what she was almost certain to experience if she had married and had kids with him.

I want to be clear that I'm not against alcohol use per se. Countless people drink in moderation with no negative affect on their lives. But many people don't have good control over their alcohol use, and unless they commit to getting effective help, they are very poor bets for a long-term relationship and marriage. I know that you don't want to overlook the red flag of alcohol abuse and end up in a relationship that makes you miserable. That being said, there are lots of high quality single nonalcoholic men who can be found in venues with alcohol.

Here are some ideas for alcohol serving venues where you might meet men.

- **Whiskey Bars and Lounges, Martini Bars, and Cigar Bars.** Many cities have Whiskey Bars and Lounges, Martini Bars, and Cigar Bars that attract lots of guys. You can just hang out and be friendly. In many of these settings you can participate in a Scotch tasting class or other kinds of tastings.

- **Wine Bars.** The same goes for Wine Bars.

- **Wine Tastings**. If you live in an urban area, there may be meetup groups focused on wine tasting. Lots of quality guys like wine, and it's easy to socialize in these settings. I get it that you can hardly go to a wine tasting and not taste any wine. Just remember to drink no more than one glass in total and also eat food.

- **Winery Tours** are fun and you'll have a chance to sample and socialize afterwards. Some wineries offer cheeses and other food and a place to picnic after the tour. My client Clarisse met her Mr. Right on a winery tour. They started talking during the tour and he asked her to join him for lunch at a nearby restaurant. They are now happily married.

- **Breweries and Brewery Tours.** Lots of men drink beer and will be found in breweries and on brewery tours.

- **Beer Making Classes** are likely to have lots of men and many will be single. Classes are great venues to get to know other class member.

- **Irish Pubs**. Many men frequent Irish Pubs. Some pubs have live Irish music nights and dancing, which can be a really fun way to meet single guys.

- **Country and Western Bars** often feature line dancing. You don't need a partner; it's lots of fun and it's easy to talk to the guy beside you.

- **Happy Hours at High End Restaurants and Hotels** are good places to socialize and meet men. Have a bite to eat at the bar. If you are friendly, men will find you approachable

- **Bar and Pub Crawls** involve bar hopping with a group from one bar or pub to another. There may be lots of single guys, but overdrinking may be the name of the game. So use caution.

- **Trivia Nights** at bars are fun. Our local pub has one every Wednesday night. People are friendly, and you have the opportunity to meet the other trivia players.

- **Karaoke Bars and Karaoke Nights.** Karaoke is a Japanese form of interactive entertainment where an amateur singer using a microphone sings along with recorded music. This is a good activity to do with a girlfriend or two. The amateur singer could be you.

Chapter 19
Guys Who Love Cars and Motorcycles

So many men love cars and/or motorcycles. You'll find these guys in many car- and motorcycle-related venues and activities — and some will be quality available men. As always, it's in your best interest to stay alert and to be friendly to any interesting-looking man. Here are some ideas.

• **Car Shows.** Check out nearby car shows. Just google "car show" and your city. Cars are, of course, the obvious topic of conversation. You can ask a guy what he thinks of a particular car - what he likes and doesn't like about it. Men who love cars almost always love to talk about them. If you live in or near New York City, consider attending the International Auto Show at the Javits Center. Two clients of one of my colleagues met amazing guys at this event. Every city of any size has at least one car show each year. Why not attend the next one?

• **Antique Car Shows and Auctions.** Lots of men attend. Many of the cars may be unfamiliar to you, so feel free to ask an attractive guy any questions on your mind.

• **Car Dealerships.** If you're in the market for a car, dealerships are natural venues to check out cars and guys at the dealership at the same time! Most men would be flattered if you asked their opinion on a car - they love to be of help. Even if you're not in the market for a car, you can still drop by car dealerships from time to time, look at the display cars and check out any men who are there. It doesn't involve a big time commitment. If you're looking for a wealthy guy, check out luxury car dealerships.

• **Waiting Areas for Car Washes and Car Repair Shops.** Men are often waiting for their cars at car washes and repair shops. Be friendly and strike up a conversation.

- **Car Maintenance Classes**. Many adult learning programs and some junior colleges offer these classes. There may be some great guys in the class, and be sure to check out the instructor!

- **Auto Parts Stores**. Men frequent these stores. If you see one you'd like to meet, smile and ask him a car-related question.

Lots of guys also love motorcycles. These days men from all income levels ride motorcycles. My cousin is a successful businessman who has a Harley which he rides on weekend excursions with his friends. He's married, but some of the guys he rides with are not.

- **Motorcycle Shows, Motorcycle Swap Meets, Motorcycle Rallies and Motorcycle Events.** These shows and events are very popular with men. You can find them by googling "motorcycle shows" and "motorcycle events" and your city or town to find them.

- **Motorcycle Shops**. Lots of guys will be looking at motorcycles, especially on weekends. I recently drove by a Harley Davidson shop on a Sunday afternoon and it was filled to the gills with men. If you want to meet a guy who loves motorcycles, this is the place to check out.

- **Sturgis Motorcycle Rally**. If you really want to meet a guy who's into motorcycles, consider attending the Sturgis Motorcycle Rally in Sturgis, North Dakota. This rally attracts over 500,000 people each August — mostly men who are from all walks of life — so you should be able to meet some who catch your fancy.

Chapter 20
Guys Who Love to Build and Fix Things

Don't you admire guys who can build and repair things? I do. Some guys have that creative skill. You may have it too, and you may or may not have pursued it. Traditionally women haven't been encouraged to develop this gift, although this may be changing for at least some of us. Whatever the reason, I know that I've always been attracted to guys who know how to build and fix things, and I think there are many women like me.

So how do you meet single guys who have this gift and skill? There are lots of ways.

- **Home Repair Guys**. Check out any guys you hire to make repairs in your home. Some of them may be available single men. If a guy is skilled, he may have figured out how to create a good income using those skills. I remember an old girlfriend of mine who ended up marrying a guy she hired to do some remodeling on her home shortly after her divorce. She's a professional, but she didn't reject him because he didn't have her education and status. He's a very intelligent guy who had built a successful remodeling business. So a word to the wise professional woman: Don't reject a great guy just because he has a job you might not consider high status enough for you. You might have a lot more in common than you think. If, however, you truly consider guys who work with their hands beneath you, you'd likely be miserable being married to one. But if you feel you can get beyond your prejudices to give some great guys a chance — guys who may be builders, contractors, painters, plumbers, etc. — you may find the love of your life, just as my old friend did.

- **Home Depot and Lowes**: These stores tend to be crawling with men who are professional builders, painters, electricians, etc. as well as with guys who are tackling home repair jobs. If you spot an attractive guy who may be single, don't be afraid to smile and ask him for help in choosing the right paint for your outdoor steps or the best light fixture for your bathroom. If he's looking around in the paint or light fixture section, he's likely to be able to help you. And who knows - he may even offer to assist you with your project. I know of more than one romance which started that way. [Safety Tip here: Use the same caution with a man you meet this way as you would before inviting any stranger into your home. Don't invite a guy you don't know reasonably well into your home when it's going to be just the two of you. Most of the time, everything will be fine, but you want to be protective of your personal safety especially with people you've just met.]

- **How-to-Workshops at Home Depot**. Many Home Depots teach how-to-workshops in various skills like lawn prep, installing floor tiles, and staining your deck. It's a great way to learn a useful new skill and guys may be teaching and taking these workshops. This is a natural way to meet a new guy who wants to improve his skills.

- **Home Shows**. Watch your local paper and check the Internet for announcements about Home Shows where home improvement vendors display their wares and their expertise. Lots of guys who are interested in home improvement or who are in some aspect of the business attend these shows. You can wander from display to display, be curious and ask questions to guys nearby.

- **Paint Stores** attract professional painters and weekend amateur painters. My dad owned a paint and wallpaper store when I was young, so I've always felt comfortable in these stores. I used to work in the store, and I remember waiting on lots and lots of guys. Check out paint stores, especially if you have a paint job of your own and want to get ideas about paint types and colors.

- **Hardware Stores** are like candy stores for many men. They can get lost there for hours just like we can get lost in clothing stores. Hardware stores are fascinating, not only because of the abundance of male shoppers, but because you'll find so many odd and interesting things for sale. Why not go to your local hardware store one Saturday or Sunday and wander around just taking in the wares while on the lookout for single handymen you might engage in casual conversation?

- **Department Store Tool Sections.** There aren't many department stores with tool sections these days, but there are some. Guys who are looking for good quality tools may be checking them out. If you're in the mall, why not take a 10-minute detour through the tool department and see if you run into a cute guy?

- **Woodworking Classes.** Interested in learning to make wood furniture and other wooden items? You may be one of the few women in your woodworking class. If this appeals to you, check out your local adult school and small woodworking businesses that may offer such classes. Google "woodworking classes" and your location to see what's available.

Chapter 21
Guys Who Love Plants and Gardening

Lots of guys love growing plants and flowers. I have had two serious boyfriends who loved gardening. The first was my high school boyfriend who worked at a nursery and gave me the most beautiful orchid corsages. Later I lived with a guy who loved to garden and who taught me a lot about it. I've always felt so grateful. If gardening is one of your passions, and you'd love to find a partner who shares it, try these venues:

- **Nurseries, Landscaping Centers and Garden Shops.** These venues are frequented by gardeners. Keep your **Man Radar** on for attractive guys when you visit these venues. It's so easy to start a conversation because you can ask if he knows anything about growing a particular plant, if he can recommend a plant that would thrive in a shady spot in your yard or a sunny spot on your deck. He'll love to help you out and if he's single and unattached, he just may offer to help you plant your garden.

- **Community Gardens**. Many urban areas have community gardens where local residents without yards may claim a spot to garden. I knew a great single guy named Ron who lived in an apartment building in my neighborhood. He really wanted to meet and marry a wonderful woman, and he did. He met her at the community garden where he was growing tomatoes and flowers, and she was growing squash, pumpkins and flowers. They've been married for 15 years and have 3 terrific kids. A community garden is a great place to get to know people, because people are often working there for extended periods of time, and you'll get to know them as you work beside them. You have an easy topic of conversation – gardening – to get the relationship started. Check out your local community garden if you want to meet a guy who loves growing plants.

- **Botanical Gardens and Arboretums** attract people who love plants, including single guys. Here again, there's an obvious topic of conversation to serve as an icebreaker. When you visit a botanical garden or an arboretum, aren't you blown away by the interesting plants? Don't you have questions about some of them? Ask that cute guy nearby. He may be delighted to engage with you.

Chapter 22
Dancing and Musical Venues

Dancing –

If you love to dance as I do, you probably agree that nothing is more fun. There are single guys wanting to meet you at most dances, so what are you waiting for? If you don't know how to dance and want to learn, there's almost always a lesson at the beginning of the evening. Sometimes men outnumber women. Even if there are more women, if you're friendly and open to the men, it's likely that you'll have a number of partners. If you're a beginner, there will almost certainly be men who are also beginners and you can practice together. I did a ton of dancing when I was single, and I never regretted one night spent dancing whether or not I had lots of partners or met anyone I wanted to date. Here are some dancing suggestions:

- **Salsa.** Salsa dancing is great fun and often attracts single men. Although Salsa may look hard to a beginner, it's actually based on one basic step. Once you learn that step, you will start learning variations on that step and are likely to be hooked.

- **Swing.** I haven't done much swing dancing, but the little I've done was really fun. My client Liz met her husband while they were both learning to swing dance. After two years of marriage, they still swing dance together at least once a week.

- **Square Dancing.** Chances are you learned square dancing when you were a kid, but may not have done it since. There are square dancing groups all over the U.S. and Canada and in other parts of the world too. It's done in sets of 4 couples with a caller calling out the steps. It takes a little while to learn the steps and patterns, but there are often lessons at the beginning of the evening, and the dancers are usually welcoming to newcomers and will help you learn the moves. If you like to dance, I think you'll enjoy it.

- **Contra Dancing.** I love love love Contra Dancing. It's a North American dance that grew out of English Country Dancing during the colonization of America. Contra dance moves are similar to square dance moves, but it's usually done in two long lines of couples. You move with your partner up and down the line and get to dance with everyone. This makes it terrific for connecting with all the men in the room.

- **Zydeco.** Zydeco Dancing comes from the Louisiana Cajun culture and has spread around the U.S. and Canada. It's done in couples to wonderful Zydeco music – often played by a live band. The music makes you want to get up and dance, and best of all, the dance isn't hard to learn. There's a basic step to master, just as in salsa, and once you've mastered it, you'll learn to improvise to your heart's content. There are strong Zydeco dance communities in a number of places, and lots of guys are hooked on it.

- **Ballroom Dancing.** There are Ballroom Dance venues and lessons in almost all urban areas. You'll learn to waltz, fox-trot, quickstep, tango, mambo, cha-cha and more. You'll meet lots of guys. Caution – you're likely to get addicted to the dancing, even if you don't find the right partner.

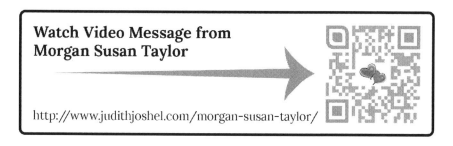

Watch Video Message from Morgan Susan Taylor

http://www.judithjoshel.com/morgan-susan-taylor/

Morgan Susan Taylor, M.A. is a spiritual healer, speaker, writer and therapist specializing in women's sexuality and feminine spirituality. She is the founder of the Feminine Wisdom Academy (www.femininewisdomacademy.com) where she helps awakening women create the intimacy they want without feeling like they have to sacrifice themselves to get it. Request your free copy of Morgan's ebook "The Pleasure Keys" at www.PleasureKeys.com.

This is the brief story of how I met my amazing man, Mark. Mark and I really met on the dance floor. I had met him once or twice kind of in passing. He's a professional ballroom dance instructor and I had briefly met him in one of his classes once and once just at a social event, but never really had any kind of a connection with him. One night I was out social dancing and Mark happened to be there too. He walked up to me and he asked me if I wanted to dance. We danced a lovely dance on the dance floor and I just remember feeling so playful and really like I could be myself. We had a great connection, and I was actually really surprised by it. We ended up just kind of really connecting and talking that night and dancing together some more and just really having so much fun together. We didn't date immediately. We got to know each other for a couple months. We were hanging out and we danced together. He turned to me one day and he said, "You know, people have been asking me who this blonde woman is I've been hanging out with and they keep asking me if we're dating. I looked at him and I said, "Well? Maybe we should date." And he said, "I'm so glad that you said something." We've been together ever since. One of the things that was so special about Mark is that we were in love with each other before we had even kissed, before we had been intimate. We also agreed to go into a committed relationship before we had even kissed. One of the biggest challenge in our relationship was the fact that I have two school aged children. My daughters are 12 and 16 currently. Mark has kids too, but they're older and they live in another country. My kids actually had a pretty tough time accepting Mark into their lives and accepting the fact that he was really going to be part of our family. Mark did an amazing job of putting up with the tough tests that they put him through. One of the things that I believe has really made our relationship successful is the fact that Mark and I are really committed to the value of growth in the relationship – personal growth and relational growth. Mark is an amazing man and whenever we have a conflict he'll always look within, he'll always pull back and examine what could I do differently or what went wrong, how did that happen? I

love that about him. I think I equally bring that into the relationship. I work to grow and see myself more clearly. I really attribute our success to the fact that both of us are really rooted and grounded in the value of growth. My best piece of advice to you is if you're really looking to find or connect with or trust your ideal partner, follow your passion. Engage in the activities and the things that you love to do. I would not have met Mark if I hadn't decided to pursue my passion and love of ballroom dancing. Ballroom dancing put me in the right setting and situation to connect with someone else who was of like mind who also had similar values and similar interests to me, and as a result we share that passion together. It's been really lovely. So if you're looking to attract your ideal man into your life, just focus on the things that you love to do. Follow your bliss. Follow your passion. That naturally will put you in the right kind of setting where you will meet people and very possibly the man who is perfect for you.

- **Israeli Dancing.** You can find Israeli Dance venues in most urban areas. Israeli dances are done in lines and in circles, sometimes with partners and sometimes without. Some dances are vigorous and athletic while others are deeply lyrical and romantic. A wide range of people attend, often including single men of all ages. My good friend Cindi met her long term boyfriend at an Israeli dance, so check it out.

- **Folk Dancing.** Many cultures have their own folk dances. You'll find folk dancing groups in large cities and in some college towns. If you live in the UK, there may be a folk dance group near you. If you think you might enjoy folk dancing, check out an international group that does dances from all over the world. There is almost always a dance lesson for beginners at the start.

- **Dance Clubs and Lounges.** There are dance clubs and lounges everywhere. Go with a girlfriend or two and check some of them out. Keep yourself safe by drinking little or no alcohol. My client Elizabeth met her husband at a club several years ago. She went there regularly with girlfriends to do world dance. Her husband-to-be also danced there with some of his friends. He and Elizabeth were both in other relationships at the time and just had fun dancing together. Several years later they discovered they were both single. They started dating and eventually married.

- **Ecstatic Dance.** Ecstatic Dance started in Hawaii as a spiritual free-form type of dance where you can move your body as you wish so long as you respect everyone around you. You can dance alone or with one or more people as you wish. Ecstatic Dancing is now done in venues all over the world. It feels great and it can be spiritual, if you want it to be. In any case, it's great exercise and lots of fun. No alcohol or drugs are allowed. I know of two women who met their husbands at Ecstatic Dances. If you're something of a free spirit, why not check it out?

Other Music Venues –

- **Live Music Venues** attract lots of single guys. Do you love **rock, country, rhythm and blues, jazz, rap, pop, electronic, folk, Latin, reggae music** and/or other kinds of music? Whatever your musical tastes, many single guys will be turned on by the kinds of music you love. Be on the lookout for **concerts, music festivals, and clubs featuring music, bands and artists you enjoy.** When you are listening to music that moves you, your energy is high and you are in a great place to attract men. Enjoy yourself and be your warm and friendly self.

- **Playing with Other Musicians.** If you enjoy playing music and and want to meet other amateur musicians to jam with, check out meetup groups in your area. Musicians you meet in these groups may be able to connect you with other musicians who get together to play for fun.

Chapter 23
Moms with Kids: Where Are the Kid-Friendly Guys?

Moms with kids often feel challenged in finding quality single men open to a relationship. Although some men are open to dating a mom for a while, they may not be interested in becoming part of a family that already exists. But lots and lots of men who really enjoy kids are totally open to dating and marrying a mom with kids. These men may either be dads themselves, or they may simply love kids and would never reject a woman because she's a mom.

These days many men have their kids living with them half-time or even full-time. Just like you, they understand that a parent's priority must be his or her kids, and they juggle finding time to date just as you do. They get it.

Where might you meet available men with kids of their own? Let's start close to home.

- **Your Child's Daycare Provider or Nursery School.** While many men with kids in daycare or nursery school may be married or otherwise attached, some are likely to be unattached and available. Keep your eyes open and observe other parents coming and going when you're dropping off and picking up your child. Be friendly to all of them. It should soon become clear who is married or otherwise attached and who is not. If after a while you're not sure about a guy's relationship status, consider asking one of the teachers if you feel s/he is someone you can trust.

- **Your Child's Elementary or Middle School.** As always, the key is to smile and be friendly to all parents you see when you drop off and pick up your kids. Strike up conversations with parents at PTA meetings, school activities like fairs and parties, and at intramural school sports activities open to parents. If you have the time, volunteer to be a parent chaperone for school outings and other activities so you can get to know your child's classmates and their parents.

- **Playgrounds.** If you have young kids, **playgrounds** are a great place to meet other parents, including single dads. While you're there watching your kids, it's easy to strike up a conversation with a dad who's also there watching his kids.

- **Single Parents Support Groups and Parents without Partners.** Chapters of these groups exist in many communities. Check them out. Single fathers need support and social connections like you do and may attend. These groups are also a great place to make female friends who are facing the challenges of raising kids on their own. You never know which of these women might be able to introduce you to a great guy or be willing to provide free babysitting for you when you go out on a date.

- **Children's Birthday Parties**. Your kids will be invited to some of their friends' birthday parties. Ask the hostess if you can stay for a while and help. This will give you the chance to meet single fathers who might also attend.

- **Soccer Practice, Soccer Games, Little League Practice, Little League Games**. Fathers often coach or participate in their kids' soccer and Little League practices and games. These can be natural venues to meet single dads. And don't forget about participating in **fundraisers** for these activities.

- **Scout Trips and Projects.** Volunteer to help. Your kid will feel supported, and you'll get to check out the parents of the other kids. Also consider becoming a **Scout, Brownie or Campfire Girls Leader**. You'll get to know the parents of all the kids in your troop.

Keep your eyes open for single dads at kid-friendly venues like:

- **Petting Zoos** and **Regular Zoos**
- **Planetariums**
- **Aquariums**

- **Water Parks**
- **Theme Parks**
- **County Fairs**
- **Christmas Tree Farms**
- **Disney World and other Disney Parks**
- **Carnivals**
- **Roller Skating and Ice Skating Rinks**
- **Orchards where you pick your own fruit**
- **Pumpkin Patches**
- **Halloween Parties and Parades**
- **Museums that appeal to kids and their dads**
- **Toy Stores and Toy Factories**
- **Bowling Alleys with Miniature Bowling Lanes**
- **Miniature Golf Courses**
- **Kite Flying Fields**
- **Kite Festivals**
- **Remote Control Plane Flying Fields**
- **Easter Egg Hunts**

A number of these venues, like zoos and museums, may have **Concession Stands, Cafes, Cafeterias, and Restaurants.** These are really good places to strike up conversations with guys who have their own kids in tow.

- **Kid-Friendly Restaurants** like Chuck E. Cheese and McDonalds. On weekends, you'll often see divorced weekend dads with their kids at kid-friendly restaurants like these and at lots of other restaurants. Many of these dads don't want to cook or they don't know how.

- **Food Venues Selling Sweets.** Just like you, single fathers may take their kids to **Ice Cream Shops, Ice Cream Trucks, Candy Shops and Chocolate Factories.**

- **Pediatrician, Dentist and Orthodontist Waiting Rooms.** Everyone has to take their kids to the doctor and the dentist. There's usually time to kill in doctors' waiting rooms, so put away your phone and your iPad and strike up a conversation with an attractive guy who's also waiting with his kid.

- **Kid-Focused Entertainment Venues**. You may find single dads and their kids at some of these venues:

  - **Magic Shows**
  - **Puppet Shows**
  - **The Nutcracker Ballet**
  - **Holiday Concerts**

- **Music and Dance Recitals.** If your kid takes music or dance lessons, you may have the opportunity to meet interesting single dads at your kid's **piano, violin or dance recital.** There's often a social gathering after the recital — the perfect place to tell a proud dad how well his kid performed. You might also see a devoted single dad dropping off or picking up his kid from a lesson.

- **Your Child's Male Teachers.** And don't forget to check out your kid's male teachers. Some of them may be single and very interested in connecting with you. You know he's into kids because he's a teacher. BUT it can be tricky dating your child's teacher, so you might want to hold off until your child moves on to the next grade. Jeff was Julie's son's third grade teacher. They had been attracted to each other all year, but neither thought the other was available. Toward the end of the school year, a mutual friend clarified Jeff and Julie's status and they began dating during summer vacation. They were married two years later. Julie's son was thrilled that his favorite teacher had become his stepdad.

Chapter 24
Guys with Cultural Interests

Would you love to meet guys who share your passion for art, great writing, theater or film? Lots of single guys are culture vultures and would love to meet a woman like you. There are venues frequented by people who love classical music and Shakespeare and other venues frequented by people interested in new edgy poetry, music or sculpture.

Visual Arts –

Visual arts don't just attract slim-hipped men dressed in tight black jeans and black silk shirts, sporting long hair and earrings. I've watched, what I assume to be single women, sidle up to guys who look as if they'd be more comfortable on a baseball field than a museum, and begin a conversation. Later, I noticed them chatting as they checked out another room in the exhibit. And the Arts don't just mean watching and listening; they also include experiencing – making art or creating music yourself. Here are some ideas:

- **Art Classes and Workshops** are great places to meet guys who want to develop their artistic talent. Try classes in drawing, painting, pottery, sculpture and photography. My friend Elisa met a great guy at an outdoor watercolor workshop and they dated for a couple years. Although their romantic relationship didn't work out over the long term, they are still good friends, and he is absolutely there for her when she needs him — as she recently did when she was recovering from surgery.

  These venues usually attract more women than men, but you will also find men there. It doesn't matter if there are more women than men in the class. If you take a seat next to a guy and direct your charming smile and conversation toward him, you're likely to beat out the competition.

- **Gallery Openings.** It's exciting to see new art exhibits, and gallery openings are often festive occasions where food and drink are served and there's opportunity for conversation. Google "art gallery openings" and "photography exhibit openings" and the name of your city and see what comes up.

- **Art Museums.** Lots of guys interested in art frequent art museums. Go at a relatively busy time to check out recent exhibits and check out guys who are there at the same time. **Museum Cafés** are great places to hang out. Take a seat near an attractive man and ask him for his opinion on the latest exhibit. It's a perfect icebreaker.

- **Art Museum Tours and Talks.** You'll find lots of art lovers at tours and lectures. Become a museum member, and you'll be invited to special events. These can be great venues to meet men who appreciate and support the arts. And some may be single and looking for you – a woman who also loves the arts.

- **Art Supply Stores** may be filled with practicing and budding artists, some of whom will be single guys.

- **Art Festivals and Shows.** These are often held outdoors, and they not only attract art lovers, but also people who enjoy the outdoors and find it pleasant to spend time outside surrounded by interesting people and different kinds of art. Ask a cute guy who's by himself what he thinks of a watercolor or a sculpture.

- **Photography Classes and Workshops and Camera Stores** are ideal venues to meet photographers and people learning photography. I have a friend Judy who's in a long-term relationship with Jack, a photographer. Judy needed to take photos of the exquisite jewelry she creates so she took a photography class from Jack. Jack offered to meet his students at a camera store to help them buy digital cameras and Judy was the only one who showed up. Jack helped her select a camera and she took him out to dinner to thank him. As Judy says, "We are now in our 14th year and still cookin'." You may be interested to know that Jack and Judy were in their 60s when they met.

Book Lovers and Writers –

- **Bookstore Browsing.** People who love to read often also love to browse in bookstores. Pop into your favorite bookstore from time to time to check out new books and any attractive guys who may be browsing. If a guy's there, you know he's a reader, and you have a natural topic of conversation. You might say, "Excuse me, I'm thinking of buying this book. Have you read it?" Or "I'm looking for something to read that will take me in a new direction. Can you recommend a book you really enjoyed?"

  Unfortunately, bookstores seem to be fading fast due to the Internet, but there are still some great independent bookstores, and Barnes and Noble hasn't bit the dust quite yet. Also - the men who work at bookstores are not only helpful but often tend to be older – and may be available.

- **Author Readings** in bookstores are natural places to meet readers. Keep an eye on the schedule of author readings at your local bookstore and drop in to readings you think may attract men. Get there a little early, and if you see a guy who interests you, grab the seat next to him. You have a natural subject of conversation – the featured author and book. Smile and ask him what he knows about the author or the book. And you'll feel more comfortable if you've done your homework and read up on the author, so you can add to the conversation.

- **Poetry Readings.** In larger cities, there's a community of people who attend poetry readings. Why not check it out? If you go a few times, you'll start recognizing familiar faces, and this community may develop into one of your communities.

- **Writing Classes** are offered in a number of colleges and are taught privately as well. If you're serious about improving your writing skills, consider enrolling. You get to know the other students because you often read your work aloud in these classes. It's a great way to learn more about a man who may interest you, and it gives you a way to engage with him.

- **Writers Workshops.** Are you an aspiring writer? If so, these are great venues to meet like-minded people. There are writers' workshops in many cities and writers' retreats are often held in spots of great natural beauty. Google "writers' workshops" and "writers' retreats" and see what comes up. There are writers' workshops and retreats for various genres — fiction, science fiction, nonfiction and various categories of fiction and nonfiction. One of my clients attended a writers' workshop and met interesting people from a variety of backgrounds, including a guy she found attractive. If you're a writer, this venue could be a goldmine for you in more ways than one.

A woman I know attended the Santa Barbara Writers' Workshop and not only met an editor from New York who had been invited to speak to the group, she also got to spend time alone with him. The result was a good contact that eventually led to his recommending an agent for her. It also led to a hot long-distance romance.

Theater and Film Lovers –

- **Acting Classes** are great fun and often attract single men. **Improvisation Classes** are particularly exciting. When I lived in Chicago, I took some improvisation classes from a couple who were Second City members and had a fabulous time, even though I can be shy. And there were several quality single guys in the class. Once you try these classes, you may be hooked.

- **Community Theater.** Are there any community theater groups in your area? Guys who love theater are involved in these groups not only as actors, but as set designers, lighting specialists, managers, and public relations. Even if you're a shy type and don't want to act, these groups need lots of behind-the-scenes help. When I was an attorney, I mediated a divorce where the man was passionately involved in his local community theater group. Shortly after the divorce finalized, he met a lovely single woman who had joined the troupe, and they ended up happily married. What better way to meet the man of your dreams?

- **Volunteer to be on the board and/or to raise money for professional as well as community theater groups**. This is a great way to meet other theater aficionados and to support your local theater. Be sure to attend the benefits and fundraisers. There is almost always a chance to socialize over drinks and refreshments. You'll meet new people with a common interest in theater.

- **Attend the Theater.** Go by yourself if you have no one to go with you. In fact, it's easier for a guy to approach you if you're alone. If you're lucky enough to be seated next to a man who's by himself, be friendly. Use the intermission to mingle with the crowd in the lobby. Strike up a conversation about the play if you see an interesting man.

- **Theater Meetup Groups.** It's fun to go to the theater with others. These groups will often meet before or after the play for a drink or a bite to eat.

- **Shakespeare Festivals.** There are Shakespeare festivals all over the U.S. and in Canada and the UK, as well. If you're nearby, why not attend? Educated literary men are likely to be there.

- **Film Festivals**. Most cities of any size have film festivals. Although watching films is a solitary activity, there may be opportunities to meet guys when you're standing in the ticket line, when you're in the lobby, or at the refreshment counter during intermission. If there's an opening reception, be sure to attend. These can be ideal venues to meet other film lovers, some of whom may be single guys.

- **Film Meetup Groups.** My friend Denise had been looking for her Mr. Right for a long time. Nothing worked out until she joined a film meetup group and met her boyfriend, Jim. This was a number of years ago and they are still happily together in a committed relationship.

Classical Music Lovers –

If you love classical music, wouldn't it be great to have a partner who shares your passion? This is very possible if you focus your attention on classical music venues and activities.

- **Classical Music Concerts** of all types attract male music lovers. Go to concerts that interest you and look around you at the audience. If you're at an amateur event with unassigned seats, see if there's a free seat next to a solo guy. Take advantage of the intermission by going to the lobby, mingling and being open to talking to people. People are usually interested in expressing their opinion about the music. Consider the following venues:

  - **Symphony Concerts and Rehearsals**. Many symphonies have rehearsals that are open to the public. It's super interesting to see how conductors work with their musicians to improve the performance. The atmosphere at rehearsals is often much more casual than at concerts, and therefore it may be easier to connect with other audience members.

  - **Opera**. You might be surprised at how many men love opera and not just older men. Because tickets are often pricey, the opera can be a good venue to meet financially successful guys. And there's a tradition at many opera houses for long intermissions where people can see and be seen. If you don't have lots of money, remember that many opera companies sell standing room only tickets at greatly reduced prices. Standing room opera fans tend to be very friendly — the fact that everyone in the standing room section is passionate enough about opera to stand through a performance creates a bond and makes it easy to start conversations.

  - **Choral Concerts**. Larger communities often have both professional and amateur choruses and choirs. I recently attended an awesome free chorale concert. Sitting next to me was a single woman who looked to be around 45 and next to her was a single guy a little older who had come alone. I heard them chatting about the performance during intermission, and then I heard him invite her to join him for a bite to eat after the concert. Was this the start of a budding romance? I don't know, but I do know that this is one way a music-loving woman can meet a music-loving man.

- **Classical Music Festivals** are annual events in some places. Lots of people attend and they are often held in outdoor venues. Sometimes lectures and rehearsals are open to the public. Go, enjoy, and keep your eyes open for single guys.

- **Playing and Singing Classical Music**. Do you play classical music? Even if you're a true amateur, you can find other musicians to play music with. Many men play classical music for fun, and they may be in musical groups who welcome other musicians. The following are possibilities to check out.

  - **Local Orchestras** are often looking for musicians and some accept everyone who applies.

  - **Small Chamber Groups**. It may take some research to find local chamber groups open to new members. Google "chamber music groups" or "classical music groups" and the name of your city. The staff at your local music store may be able to turn you on to a local chamber group. They also may have a bulletin board where people can advertise for musicians. And don't forget to check your local meetup groups. If you don't find anything promising, remember that you can start a group yourself on meetup.com or simply on your own.

  - **Choirs and Choruses:** If you love to sing, consider joining a singing group that sings music you are passionate about. Possibilities are **church choirs** and **community choruses**. Although singing groups usually have more female members, there will be some men who love to sing and some are likely to be single. If you're friendly, you can get to know them all over time. Choirs and choruses are also great places to make new female friends and your new girlfriend from your chorus may know just the right guy for you.

Chapter 25
Men of Your Religious Faith

Where do you find religious men? They are everywhere, but you'll meet them particularly in places of worship. Congregants are usually welcoming. As you gradually get to know members, let the ones you're comfortable with know that you'd love to meet a quality guy who shares your faith. If they know anyone, they're likely to introduce you.

In larger cities, different churches, temples, and mosques appeal to different age groups. For example, a Gothic Congregational Church in downtown Los Angeles seems to draw a younger crowd of late twenty and thirty somethings. And their Christmas midnight service and Easter service draws people from all over L.A.

Here are more ideas:

- **Religious Services**. Attend religious services regularly, not just at your own church or synagogue. Even if, at first, you have no success in meeting guys, be willing to return to a particular church or synagogue several times.

- **Small Church or Synagogue Groups.** Every church and synagogue has small groups focusing on different topics and activities. These groups are great places to meet members and really get to know them. There may be interesting single men in the group. If not, you'll be making new friends of your faith, and one of them may know the perfect guy for you.

  Many churches and temples also have community outreach programs where a small group of members may interact with various community groups to work on issues such as homelessness.

- **Girlfriends of Your Faith**. Making girlfriends who share your faith is a powerful way to meet men of your faith. I met my husband through my Jewish girlfriends. The same thing happened for a number of my friends. Nurture and cherish your girlfriends.

- **Denominational Events**. Attend Christian, Jewish or Muslim events. It might be a concert, a festival, a talk, or a class. You're likely to have fun and meet new people.

- **Graduate Programs at Denominational Colleges**. If you want to pursue a graduate degree, consider enrolling in a school with your religious affiliation. There will be many men of your faith there who are also pursuing graduate degrees.

- **Singles Christian and Jewish Meetup Groups.** Check your local meetups for singles groups of different denominations. They can be good places to meet compatible Christian or Jewish guys. If there is more than one, try them all.

- **Church Singles Groups**. Many churches have singles groups that sponsor various activities for singles. I've heard complaints from women about the number and quality of men in these venues, but I do know that some of these venues are good places to meet good men. If you're looking for a Christian man, google the name of your denomination and singles groups and see what comes up.

- **Catholic Alumni Clubs International.** These clubs exist in cities all over the U.S. They are for single Catholics who have had some college education, and they sponsor various events. Many of their members are professionals. There are 30 chapters in the U.S. and they host a yearly national convention. If you want to meet a Catholic guy, this is a great resource for you. You can find more information at caci.org.

- **Jewbilee in San Francisco**. This group was started in 2016 by two Jewish brothers who didn't like the Internet dating scene or meeting women on dating apps. It's focused on Jewish singles in their 20s and 30s who want to meet single Jews in person. The group hosts monthly parties you can learn about by visiting their Facebook page. You can also learn about other events going on the Bay Area that might interest you. A similar group **Gin and Jews in Boston** hosts parties in bars and other social and cultural events for young Jews.

- **Create a Group for Singles of Your Faith**. If you can't find a good venue to meet single men of your faith, why don't you and your girlfriends create one? Use Jewbilee or Gin and Jews as your model. You don't have to include alcohol at your events if you don't want to. You will be giving yourself and singles like you a tremendous gift by creating a new way to meet each other.

Chapter 26
Spiritual Men

Many spiritual women want to meet a man who is on the same path. If you are seeking a spiritual soul mate, I urge you to think more expansively about spirituality. My colleague and friend, Nijole Sparkis spoke about this when I interviewed her and I'd like to share with you what she told me:

"Many men who would never practice yoga or meditation find deep spirituality in nature and in physical activities like running, skiing and team sports, and in artistic expression such as music and art. These men may be just as spiritual as you, but they connect with their spirituality in different ways." I challenge you to expand your definition of spirituality so that you don't reject fabulous men who are spiritual in their own ways.

That being said, there are increasing numbers of men who meditate, practice yoga and pursue other spiritual disciplines. You can meet them by pursuing similar spiritual activities and practices.

Here are some ideas on where to meet spiritual men:

- **Yoga Classes**. Yoga classes attract many single men these days. Some are there for the physical benefits, but many have a spiritual attraction to yoga. In any urban area, there will be various types of yoga classes offered. Younger men are apt to attend the more physically vigorous types of yoga practice like **Iyengar Yoga, Ashtanga Yoga, Power Yoga, and Hot Yoga**.

   But older men love yoga too. A man I know in his late sixties attends yoga classes three times a week and met his current girlfriend after one of the classes. Get to class early and place your mat next to an attractive guy. Smile, say hi.

- **Meditation Classes and Groups.** Different types of meditation are available in different locales. Google "meditation classes" and the name of your nearest city and various possibilities will come up. Experiment with different meditation practices and see what resonates with you and whether any of your fellow meditators are attractive men who may be single. When you meditate with a group for a while, you'll start to form bonds with other meditators. Some of my friends and clients are deeply involved in **Buddhist meditation** and feel that it has had a profoundly positive influence on their lives. Lots of men are attracted to it. There are different types of Buddhist meditation, including **Zen, Tibetan, Triratna and Kadampa**, among others. Many people who don't consider themselves particularly spiritual learn **Transcendental Meditation** to help them with anxiety and focusing their minds or **Mindfulness-Based Stress Reduction Meditation** whose name says it all. I've done the **Chinese meditation practices of tai chi and qi gong** and both types of practices attract men. Tai chi and qi gong have a martial arts component but are often practiced as moving meditations without a martial arts focus.

- **Meditation Studios**. Meditation studios are popping up in U.S. cities these days. They are welcoming spaces that offer various kinds of meditation classes. Some also offer a place to sit quietly and do your own meditation. These studios are likely to attract high-powered guys seeking a way to unplug and relax for a little while. You just might connect with one of them after a class.

- **Personal and Spiritual Growth Workshops** are widely available. They are of varying quality so you'll want to do your due diligence before signing up. Men, as well as women, like these workshops, and they can be places to meet quality guys. [*A word to the wise: Some of these workshops encourage touch and the expression of at least some sexuality and women may not feel safe. So be sure to do your homework before signing up, especially if you'll be staying overnight.*]

Watch Video Message from Debbieanne DeRose

http://www.judithjoshel.com/debbianne-derose/

Debbianne is an uplifting Author, Speaker and MENtor to conscious creators worldwide. With humor and love, she brings airy-fairy concepts down to Earth — where you can use them! In 2012, Debbianne MANifested the Man of Her Dreams, and she's been inspiring and MENtoring single gals to MANifest theirs ever since.

I met the man of my dreams at a meditation retreat. Well it's more than a meditation retreat, it's a consciousness exploration program. The short story is that I went for the spoon bending and I ended up spooning with the man of my dreams. Spoon bending is probably not your thing or maybe it is. It's not for everyone. The point is I was doing something I was excited about and that's the ticket – whatever floats your boat, whatever is exciting to you, whatever makes you happy, that's the thing to do because then you're in happy vibrations. I was intrigued by all the programs they offered there, especially spoon bending, and I ended up meeting this amazing man, Tony, who's into the same thing. Follow your bliss, follow your highest excitement because it is a vibrational thing. Don't do things you don't want to do. People tell you have to do online dating. No, you don't have to that, you don't have to do anything. Just be yourself, be happy. It's all an inside job!

http://www.debbianne.com/manifesting-love-loa/

- **Retreat Centers.** Consider a rejuvenating trip to a retreat center. These centers offer many kinds of programs that may interest you. Look particularly for programs that are likely to attract men. Four well-known retreat centers to check out are the **Esalen Institute in Big Sur, CA, The Omega Institute in Rhinebeck, NY, Shambhala Mountain Center in the Colorado Rockies and the Feathered Pipe Ranch in Montana,** and there are many more you'll find by googling "Spiritual Retreat Centers".

Glen — Eyrie.

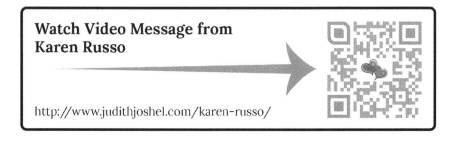

Watch Video Message from Karen Russo

http://www.judithjoshel.com/karen-russo/

Karen Russo is your Money Momentum Coach. Her signature creation is CFO Camp: 90 Days to Clarity, Confidence and Cash Flow for the Financial Leader in all of Us. Karen is the global leader of the online Money Keys Community where business owners, creative types, coaches, healers and spiritual seekers lead money lives that are peaceful, creative, generous, prosperous and free! Karen is also the award-winning author of The Money Keys: Unlocking Peace, Freedom and Real Financial Power and Grow Yourself Grow Your Wealth: Prosperity Practices for Faith and Focus, endorsed by her teachers Dr. Michael Bernard Beckwith, Katherine Woodward Thomas, and T. Harv Eker, with a foreword by Bob Proctor.

Hey dear ones, it's Karen Russo. I'm the author of "The Money Keys" and I love sharing the story of meeting the big fella. I was single and complaining about it until I was 40 even though I'd been through all this spiritual counseling training and 12 step support group stuff. I kind of knew the spiritual approach to love was to love and accept myself first. It wasn't easy for me. When I was 40, I was living in LA and I would go up to the

Big Sur Esalen Retreat Center two or three times a year, which is typically the place where you meet Mr. Right Now, not Mr. Right. And I met this fascinating interesting guy, but come on, he was ten years older, living in Arizona. He had just separated from his second wife and was really interested in being on his own. And he turned out of course to be my big fella, my twin flame. We did three years long distance, me in LA and him in Arizona. He had to finish his divorce. I had to finish ministerial school. It was not how you'd draw it up, right? – in terms of the specs. But the heart was there and the values were there. That's my encouragement to all women who are really longing for a partnership that really celebrates the very best of who you are. Trust the process. Trust yourself. Know that you are loved and I know it happens for you.

http://www.3MoneyMythsKit.com

- **New Age Bookstores** are good places to keep your eyes open for guys with spiritual interests. Also check out the **spirituality, meditation and New Age sections in regular bookstores.** A guy who's browsing books on spirituality or meditation will likely be open to talking about his interest. Ask him if he knows anything about a certain type of yoga or meditation.

Chapter 27
Animal-Loving Men

You're totally into your cats, and you want your Mr. Right to love them as much as you do. Or you may have a dog and would be oh so open to meeting a guy with a dog of his own. Here are some ideas on how to meet men who love animals.

- **Dog Walking**. Walking a dog happens to be a terrific way to meet men. If you don't have a dog, borrow one from a friend. When you're out with your dog in your own neighborhood, be friendly to attractive guys you see. If a guy is drawn to you, it's easy for him to start a conversation by asking you something about your dog, especially when the two of you stop to allow your pets to check each other out. And a guy walking his dog usually loves to be asked about his dog and will appreciate an admiring comment. Ask the dog's name and about the breed, and he can then easily ask you about your dog. My friend Chris met her beloved while she was walking her dog in her neighborhood. My client Alicia is in a serious relationship with a guy she met while walking her poodle in the park.

- This may surprise you, but some single guys consciously try to meet women through their dogs. My neighbor just told me that her 29-year-old son Matthew was having trouble meeting women. So he got a dog and takes her everywhere. He's found that if he takes his dog to a restaurant or bar with outdoor seating, the dog is a magnet for attracting women. If you have a dog, how about trying this strategy to meet men?

- **Cat Walking.** Yes cat walking. I met a long-term boyfriend while walking my cat Emily on a leash in the park. Emily kept getting herself into dangerous situations whenever I let her out, so finally I started walking her on a leash. Who knew my cat would lead me to a really great guy?

- **Dog Parks**. Dog parks in urban areas attract lots of dog owners, and they're good settings to meet unattached dog-loving men. When you're standing around watching your dog play or throwing balls for him, it's easy to strike up conversations with other dog owners. Hit the dog park at different times — particularly during dinner hour, early evenings and on weekends when employed men are likely to be there. When you see the same guy there with his dog several times, you begin to feel as if you know each other, and it's easier to start a conversation.

- **Playing Frisbie or Ball with Your Dog**. Play with your dog in any park that allows dogs and you're likely to attract attention, including attention from single unattached men.

- **Dog Meetup Groups**. Google "meetup groups dogs" and you may be surprised at the number of groups that come up. In the San Francisco Bay Area where I live, there are currently meetup groups for people with: specific dog breeds, small dogs, mutts, agile dogs, squish-faced dogs and rescued dogs. There are groups for hikers with dogs and wine lovers with dogs. Dogs are so loving and spontaneous. If you're a dog lover, having dogs around will tend to help you feel relaxed and friendly. And dogs always provide a ready-made conversation topic. If there aren't any meetup groups in your area for people with dogs, start one. It's easy.

- **Animal Rescue Groups and Facilities**. Animal-loving guys are likely to volunteer at these are venues and some will be single and available. Check out groups dedicated to rescuing specific dog breeds as well as wildlife rescue centers, marine wildlife rescue centers, and bird rescue and rehabilitation centers. And don't forget Brianne and Bill in Chapter 3 who met while volunteering to walk dogs for Southeastern Guide Dogs in Florida.

- **Vet Waiting Rooms**. When you're at the veterinarian's with your pet, check out the other pet lovers in the waiting room. Sit down near a guy who appeals to you. It's easy to smile and ask him about his cat or dog or iguana.

- **Dog Shows,** of course, attract dog lovers. If you see an interesting-looking guy who is alone, sit near him. You'll find plenty to discuss at these fascinating shows. Also go behind the scenes if you can and talk to the dog owners who are exhibiting their dogs. They are often very friendly and appreciative of your interest in their dogs – and who knows – some of them might be high quality single men.

- **Pet Supply Stores**. Pet lovers frequent these stores. Whenever you're there, be aware of the other customers and if you see an interesting-looking guy, smile and ask him a question - it might be about a brand of dog food, a type of collar or anything that comes to mind.

- **Exotic Pet Shows**. If you're interested in meeting a guy who loves birds, reptiles or fish, he may be at one of these shows.

- **Dog Training Volunteer**. There are a number of organizations that train dogs for the blind, deaf, and/or disabled and they usually need volunteers to work with the dogs. Volunteers socialize puppies and walk and train dogs. If you're a dog lover, these are very satisfying places to volunteer, and dog-loving single men may also be volunteering.

Chapter 28
Physically Fit and Health Conscious Guys

Physically fit guys and health conscious guys often participate in various sports. Chapter 16 is filled with suggestions about where to meet them. Here are some additional ideas:

- **Gyms, Health Clubs and Fitness Centers**. These are great places to find fit men and men working on becoming fit. Lots of romances start in places like these. One of my male clients recently met a woman he's interested in at the gym. Choose a workout machine next to an attractive man and smile at him. Better yet, ask for help in adjusting a machine. It might spark a conversation and an invitation for a date. Even if you're shy, a gym or a health club can be a good place to meet guys. If you go regularly, you start to notice guys who also go regularly, and it becomes easier to smile and say hi when you've seen someone several times. If you're looking for working guys, go very early in the morning and during the dinner hour/early evening. Lots of retired and semi-retired men work out, and you can find these guys at the gym throughout the day.

Watch Video Message from Victoria Thornton

http://www.judithjoshel.com/victoria-thornton/

Victoria Thornton is a Speaker, Author and Life Strategist. She helps women feel happiness from the inside out through Confidence, Clarity and Courage. She is certified through Robbins-Madanes Strategic Intervention and Jack Canfield Success Principles. She is the creator of Uncover Your Diamond online program and Big Bold Vision workshops.

As a successful entrepreneur, she is also the owner of Mind to Motion Pilates studio and certifies new Pilates Teachers.

Today I want to share with you how I met my husband. We were at a gym. He worked there and I just started. They assigned me to him as a personal trainer. Well, he sat me down and asked me what my goals were and I told him, "I want to look good in a bikini." He said, "Ok, I think we can do that." After one session I wasn't going to work with him any more and he wanted to get to know me more so he designed a contest and made sure that I won it so that I could get 4 or 5 sessions with a personal trainer and of course it was him! So we got to know each other a little bit more and really started to realize we enjoyed each other's company and had a lot of laughs. I had a 5 year old at the time and I wasn't really in the market for meeting anyone new. I wasn't really interested, but we just laughed so much and had such a good time together that pretty soon it kind of developed into more and I ended up working there. Then we both left there and started our own business. I became a personal trainer and then a Pilates instructor. We opened our own Pilates studio. We got married 17 years ago. He helped me raise my daughter, and she's getting married soon so that's pretty fun. It's just been quite a ride! I just wanted to share with you that you can meet somebody special in all different kinds of places. And you just never know. So you need to stay open to the idea. I think sometimes when we want to meet somebody, the brain says, "There are no good guys out there." Well, there are. There are lots of them and they just might be looking for you. I just want you to know that you can find your perfect mate.

http://www.VictoriaThornton.com

- **Vitamin Shops**. Guys who are into nutrition may frequent vitamin shops and stores like **GMC Nutrition**. They also may be browsing in the vitamin and supplement sections of grocery stores like **Whole Foods** and in **pharmacies**. You can always ask a man whether he's tried or can recommend a certain product.

- **Vegan Restaurants and Juice Bars** attract vegan men, so frequent these venues if you'd like to meet one. You'll probably find that you have more than the food in common.

- **Farmers Markets** attract people interested in healthy food. Some farmers markets feature live music and have an area where you can sit and listen. Shoppers at farmers markets are often in a good mood and very approachable. They often love to talk about the produce, don't be afraid to ask a cute guy whether he's tried the heirloom tomatoes.

- **Vegetarian Co-ops**. Vegetarian co-ops buy organic produce directly from farmers and sell it to their members. Guys into healthy eating may belong to one. Volunteer to pick up, sort, and distribute the produce, and you'll meet the members.

Chapter 29
Guys Interested in the Environment

Many awesome men have deep concerns about the environment. There are lots of ways to meet them.

- **Sierra Club**. Join the Sierra Club if you're in the U.S. or another environmental organization if there are no Sierra Club chapters near you. Get involved in one or more of their causes. There are likely to be some high quality men involved, and some may be single. Many areas have **Sierra Club Singles** groups – perfect for meeting single guys who love outdoor activities and are concerned about the environment. Join **Sierra Club** hikes and other outdoor activities they sponsor. The more challenging the activity, the more guys are likely to be participants. See Chapter 17 for more ideas on where to meet guys who love being out in nature.

- **Other Organizations Protecting the Environment.** Who would guess that Wikipedia has an extensive list of local, national and international organizations that focus on some aspect of protecting the environment? If you're passionate about this issue, check out the list and some of the groups that speak to your passion. You can find organizations working close to your home, as well as nationally and internationally. Many men are involved in these organizations. Some have a passion for saving wildlife, while others are deeply concerned about global warming. These organizations, especially if they have local chapters, are good bets to meet such men.

- **Shoreline Cleanup**. In areas with bodies of water, there may be designated days of shoreline cleanup. Lots of people concerned about the beauty of their environment volunteer for this activity. In the area where I live, there's a shoreline cleanup on a Saturday once or twice a year. I learned about it from a sign. Look for notices on roads. If you don't see any, google "Shoreline Cleanup" and an area description like "East Bay" or the name of a town, city, river, lake or beach and see what comes up.

WHERE ARE THE GOOD GUYS?

- **Trail Maintenance**. There are trail maintenance days open to volunteers in many local, state and national parks and recreation areas. Men who are into environmental preservation and hiking will volunteer. Working beside a guy is a great way to meet and connect with him. Plus you're doing a public service, and you'll feel good about yourself for volunteering.

Chapter 30
Generous Men

Is it important to you that your Mr. Right has a generous heart and gives back to the world? If it is, consider looking for him at volunteer activities that are likely to interest him. Would he want to help feed the homeless? Would he want to rescue animals? Would he want to tutor or mentor kids? Would he want to help people who are dying? Is he concerned about finding a cure for cancer? Does he want to help save the environment?

You can research local volunteer opportunities online. Google the name of the city and the word "volunteer" and lots of possibilities should come up. Ask yourself which of these volunteer opportunities interest you and which you think might interest your Mr. Right?

Here are some specific ideas.

- **Habitat for Humanity** volunteers build and repair housing in poor areas. These projects attract men with a heart who have building skills. But it also attracts guys who want to work with others in this way. You don't have to have any specific skills. You'll be assigned jobs at your level. One guy I know, without noticeable skills, was assigned to work on a fence for the day. There's no better way of getting to know a guy than working beside him.

- **Amnesty International** attracts people who are deeply concerned about justice and human rights. There are a number of volunteer opportunities, including those for young professionals living in larger U.S. cities. Amnesty International is also active in Australia.

- **Junior Achievement** volunteers teach kids about financial literacy, work and business.

- **Big Brothers and Big Sisters** volunteers mentor at-risk teens.

The Big Brothers and Big Sisters chapters have joint events where you can meet other volunteers. What a great way to make a difference in the world and meet dedicated male volunteers at the same time.

- **The American Red Cross** has lots of volunteer opportunities. I know a couple who met as Red Cross volunteers in New York in the aftermath of 9/11.

- **Charity Bike Rides and Races**. If you like bike riding or running, Google "Charity Bike Rides" and "Charity Races" to learn about local events in your areas. These events are likely to attract male bicyclists and runners who have a heart.

- **singlevolunteers.com.** Some communities have a Singles Volunteers chapter that will help you connect with volunteer opportunities where you can meet quality single men.

- **Food Banks** and **Serving Meals to the Homeless** attract many volunteers, including single men. You usually don't have to make a big time commitment, so if these venues interest you, check out several before making your choice.

- **Public Broadcasting Fundraising Events**. PBS stations are often looking for volunteers to answer phones during fundraisers. Quality single guys who love PBS will be among the volunteers.

- **Volunteer Tutors and Coaches** are often needed in public schools. You can make a real difference in a kid's life and connect with other volunteers and with teachers, as well. I have a male friend who volunteered as a tutor in the public schools for years.

- **Holiday Toy Drives**. Guys who love kids are likely to volunteer. Sometimes local fire and police departments are involved. These departments have lots of male employees, who, as a bonus, are usually in good physical shape.

- **Charity Events**. Look for opportunities to volunteer for charity events. It will get you behind the scenes and give you the chance to meet other volunteers involved with the charity. Some may be quality single guys.

- **Rotary Clubs**. See the discussion in Chapter 15. There are Rotary Clubs all over the world and they often have more male than female members. They are filled with civic-minded people in your local community. The meetings are great places to socialize and build relationships. Rotary Clubs are serious about giving back to their communities and offer great volunteer opportunities to their members.

- **Fundraisers**. Many nonprofit organizations have fundraising events and often need volunteers. Keep your eyes open for organizations in your area that you support and volunteer to help out. You never know whom you might meet.

- **Hospice**. Does being a hospice volunteer working with the dying seem like an unlikely activity to meet Mr. Right? I suspect you answered yes. Let me tell you about my friends Ann and John who met while training to be hospice volunteers and have been happily married for 15 years now. Their mutual interest in helping the dying showed them very early on that their values were compatible for a lifetime together.

- **Aids Walks and Rides**. There are annual walks and bike rides to raise awareness of Aids and money for its cure. All sorts of people participate, and it's super easy to meet them.

- **Other Charity Walks and Rides**. There are also walks and rides to raise money for the research and treatment of cancer, MS, Diabetes and other diseases and conditions. To learn about them Google "charity ride" and "charity walk" and the name of your city.

Chapter 31
Guys Interested in Politics

If you're interested in politics and want to meet like-minded men, you're in luck because you'll have lots of options.

- **National Political Parties and Candidates**. Volunteer for the political party and candidates you support, particularly for work that will bring you in contact with other supporters.

- **National Issues.** Research **organizations that support issues important to you,** such as combatting climate change, protecting legal rights, or gun control. These organizations are now part of almost all communities. Volunteer and work with others to bring about change on the issue that drives you. There are organizations on all sides of the political spectrum working to bring about change on particular issues and many volunteers are likely to be male. Be sure to attend **fundraisers** and other events sponsored by your organization.

- **Local Elections and Issues**. Work on a local issue such as cleaning up your local river, planting trees on city streets or creating a dog park. It will bring you in contact with your politically active neighbors. My former landlord Jim met Annette, his long-term girlfriend, through their neighborhood watch association.

- **Work at the Polls.** I've worked at the polls in several elections. At the last national election, my friend and I were poll watchers, making sure that people who were registered to vote were not turned away. We were supervised by a very high quality single guy, also volunteering. My friend and I are both married, so we weren't interested in initiating a romantic connection, but we agreed that if we had been single, there was more than one opportunity to flirt with some quality single guys.

- **Political Rallies and Marches.** Exercise your free assembly and speech rights and keep an eye out for Mr. Right at the same time. My happily married friends, Florence and John, met at an Anti-Vietnam War march in the 70s.

Chapter 32
Smart Guys

There are lots of ways to meet smart guys. Here are just a few.

- **Mensa**. Mensa is an organization of people with very high IQs. You actually have to pass an IQ test to become a member. If you pass the test, you can join, and you'll have access to lots of very smart guys. Be aware, however, that some Mensa members are snobby about their intelligence, and this may not be your cup of tea. But there are bound to be a number of more modest members who will engage and entertain you with their intelligence. Mensa holds annual social weekends for their members, as well as get-togethers in various cities.

- **Universities and Colleges.** Hang out in campus coffee shops, attend campus lectures and concerts and other events and take a class if you're not already a student. If you're not college age, remember that many of the instructors and professors won't be either and people who are older often attend events on campus.

- **College Alumni Clubs** are great places to meet college-educated men. If there's an alumni club in your area for the college you attended, be sure to check it out. Even if you don't meet any eligible men, you'll meet other graduates of your school, and they may know educated men to whom they'd be happy to introduce you.

- **Graduate School**. If you'd like to further your education, consider attending graduate school. Side benefits are that you will meet a new community of grad students and faculty, and new avenues to meet intelligent men will open up to you.

- **Libraries**. Men who love to read can be found in libraries — from public libraries to specialized libraries for law, medicine, engineering and other disciplines. If there are such libraries in your area, check them out. People reading in libraries often take breaks in nearby coffee houses or cafes, so these are good venues to find a guy taking a library coffee break.

- **Chess Clubs**. Many smart guys love chess. Google "chess club" and the name of your city. Visit your local chess club to see who's there and whether it's a game you'd like to learn if you don't already know how to play.

- **Geeks.** Geeky guys often make great husbands. There are tons of venues where geeks hang out. Any activities related to technology, math, science, robotics, gaming, computers, and finance will attract lots of geeks. Meetup groups focused in these areas are great places to meet such men.

Chapter 33
Rich Guys

If you want to marry a rich guy, your best bet is to frequent venues that wealthy people frequent. Here are some ideas:

- **Toney Neighborhoods.** If you don't live in a toney neighborhood, but there's one nearby, frequent the businesses and amenities in the toney area. Walk your dog there. Play tennis there. Eat at the restaurants.

- **Country Clubs**. Join a country club with wealthy members if you can afford it and can secure an invitation. If not, maybe you know someone who belongs who might invite you to some of the club events.

- **Yacht Clubs**. I know a woman who hangs out at yacht clubs. She's not wealthy and isn't a member, but she loves boats and has gotten to know many of the club members. She is often invited to crew on a boat and later joins everyone for drinks or dinner. She's met several men she's dated this way. [*Caveat: For your safety, never go out on a boat with anyone you don't know reasonably well and trust.*]

- **Marinas and Marina Restaurants.** Since guys with boats are often at marinas and marina restaurants, these can be good places to meet them.

- **High End Menswear Shops**. Wander through high end menswear stores like Prada and keep an eye out for an attractive guy. Ask for his opinion about a tie you're thinking of buying for your uncle.

- **Dealerships for Boats and Expensive Cars**. Cars and boats are toys for lots of men, particularly men with money. You'll run into these guys at dealerships.

- **Auctions for Anything Expensive.** The same goes for auctions for boats, classic cars, antiques and art. Some wealthy men are collectors and frequent auctions of the toys of their choice.

- **Charity Benefits and Events.** Wealthy men with social consciences are often involved with charities, so you will find them at benefits and other charity events. Check out charity events for your local opera, symphony, and museums. I have a client who met her beloved at a charity auction for a local art museum. She found herself sitting next to him by chance. He had sat down beside her, and as he knew a lot about some of the items being auctioned, he was delighted to share his knowledge with her. That was 5 years ago, and they've been happily married for the last 3 years.

- **First or Business Class.** Fly first or business class if you can afford it. Sometimes you can get bumped up to first class without paying extra.

- **First Class Airport Lounge.** If you are flying first class, you'll be able to use the First Class Lounge. While you're waiting is a great time to strike up a conversation.

Chapter 34
Financially Aware Guys

If you'd like to meet a guy who's well off or at least trying to improve his financial situation why not consider the following?

- **Shareholder Meetings.** Corporations have annual shareholder meetings. Some are elaborate affairs with food and drink and opportunities to socialize with other shareholders. Warren Buffet hosts an impressive several-day affair in Nebraska each year for shareholders in **Berkshire Hathaway**. You have to own a share to participate, and the cost can be pricey. However, you may be able to purchase a credential to attend for a minimal cost on ebay. Other shareholder meetings to check out include **Walmart, Apple, Google, Starbucks and Peets**.

- **Finance or Investment Class.** A finance or investment class taught by someone respected in the field is likely to attract men serious about investing. Try to sit next to a cute one and ask him if he has an investment tip he would share with you.

Chapter 35
Guys of a Certain Nationality

American women born in the United States and foreign-born women are often interested in meeting guys from other countries. Just the thought of a French accent is enough to turn on some women. Foreign-born women may be interested not only in meeting men from their particular countries of origin, but may also be curious about men from other countries. So, if you want to meet a man who is French or English, African, Mexican or Latin-American where might you go? Where would you go if you want to meet a South Asian or a Chinese man?

- **Embassies and Consulates** can provide opportunities to meet men from particular countries. For example, there's a French American Cultural Society connected to the French consulate in San Francisco which sponsors events and fundraisers. If you live in or near a major city, there may be embassies or consulates of various countries. Google the country, your city and consulate or embassy and see what comes up.

- **Ethnic Restaurants**. You're likely to meet Spanish people in a restaurant serving Spanish cuisine, so choose the nationality which interests you and see if there are any restaurants serving food from the region in your area.

- **Art Exhibits.** Chinese people are likely to attend exhibits of Chinese artists, especially of Chinese artists from China, such as Wei Wei. Keep your eyes open for exhibits featuring artistic works from the countries that interest you. Go to the exhibit opening where there are usually lots of people and a chance to socialize. Or go at a busy time like the weekend and be sure to visit the museum café if the exhibit is in a museum.

- **Foreign Language Meetup Groups and Classes**. In many cities, there are meetup groups for people who already speak or who want to improve their skill in a particular language like

Spanish, French, Mandarin Chinese, or Italian. There are also language classes taught in various venues. If you'd like to meet a guy who speaks a certain language, check out **adult schools and classes at local community centers and colleges**. Language conversation classes are conducive to meeting and conversing with new people and sometimes those conversations lead to relationships outside of class.

My friend Pat loved practicing her Spanish and often took classes in Spanish conversation and literature. She met several Spanish-speaking men in her classes and had a long-term relationship with one of them. It ultimately didn't work out for them because he had to return to his home country Peru for business reasons, and she decided she didn't want to leave her kids and grandkids in the U.S. It was a bittersweet parting. But then something wonderful happened for her. An old friend fixed Pat up with her brother who was recently widowed, and they ended up happily married. And guess what — her husband is also fluent in Spanish.

- **Ethnic Festivals**. Ethnic communities host festivals and events that celebrate their cultures. There are Greek, Italian, German and/or Russian festivals in many cities. Again, let Google be your guide to these festivals.

Chapter 36
Doctors and Lawyers

Lawyers

I'm a lawyer myself, and I have several thoughts on how to meet single male lawyers. Think about where lawyers might hang out and go there. Here are some ideas:

- **Courthouses and City Halls.** These venues are filled with lawyers. If you're free on a weekday, go to the courthouse and watch some trials. Don't be afraid to smile and ask an attractive attorney near you a question about the trial. Attorneys are likely to be everywhere — hanging out in the hallways, at the snack stand, sitting outside of courtrooms, standing in line to file papers and so on.

- **Restaurants, Cafes and Bars Near Courthouses and City Halls**. These venues will be filled with lawyers at lunch and even dinner and if they are open for breakfast, many of their patrons will be lawyers. Use your smile and your charm and speak to guys who look interesting.

- **Jury Duty.** As mentioned in Chapter 10, jury duty can be a good way to meet and get to know men who may interest you. When you're on jury duty, you may be waiting at the courthouse for significant periods of time. Look around for attractive male jurors and take a seat beside one. You are both killing time waiting and it's a great time to get to know someone new.

- **Law Libraries.** You'll find lawyers and law students doing research at law libraries. There are law libraries in all law schools and also in many courthouses and city halls.

Doctors

- **Hospitals** are of course filled with doctors and other medical professionals. A good place to meet them is in the **hospital**

cafeteria. Sit down near a guy wearing a lab coat and be friendly.

- **Restaurants, Cafes and Bars Near Hospitals** are often frequented by doctors. Many doctors have their offices near hospitals. They will be found in nearby eating places and cafes.

Chapter 37
Meeting Men While Traveling

Whether you're traveling for business or pleasure, there are lots of opportunities to meet men. Take your eyes off your phone, be aware of the people around you and be willing to smile at interesting-looking guys. Say something to guys you'd like to meet. Don't get hung up on what to say — almost anything will do. If a guy's interested, he'll be flattered and will pick up the ball. Be aware of any men nearby in the following arenas while you're traveling:

- **To and From the Airport.** If you're taking a van with other passengers or taking public transportation to the airport, there may be a man who catches your eye. Don't be shy. If there's an empty seat next to him, sit down, make eye contact and smile. "Where are you off to?" is a good icebreaker.

- **At the Airport.** People gather in airports at a number of places. Conversations are easy to start when you're standing in the **ticket line,** the **baggage drop off line** and the **security line**. There may be hours of waiting at the airport. Be aware of attractive guys **in line for coffee** and sitting near you at an **airport restaurant or bar**. You can ask a guy next to you a question about a book or magazine at the **magazine stand**. There also may be shops near your gate where you can kill time before your plane departs. Check out shops that may particularly attract men like **bookstores, men's clothing shops** and **stores selling tech-related items**. Then there's the **waiting area near the gate** and the **boarding line**. All these places give you opportunities to casually talk to strangers.

Not all airlines have assigned seats. **Southwest Airlines as of the writing of this book has no seat assignments**. That's great because it gives you the chance to choose any open seat you want. Why not sit down next to that cute guy you noticed in the waiting area? Even if you're flying on an airline with seat assignments, you might find yourself seated next to an appealing guy. I know a couple who met just that way on a flight from Philadelphia to San Francisco and they've been happily married for 12 years.

If you're traveling internationally, don't forget the **duty free shop**. Many people shop there before boarding their international flights. And finally there's the **baggage claim area**. Yes people in the baggage claim area are focused on finding their bags and leaving, but there's often a wait for your baggage and time for a casual flirtation with a guy who's also waiting for his luggage.

Traveling on Your Own. Whether you're traveling on your own or with a girlfriend or two, you can meet men everywhere you go. Just use safety precautions about accompanying a guy you barely know to an unknown location. Be particularly careful if you are in a country where you don't know the language and where the culture is patriarchal. That being said, you can meet quality guys in all sorts of places when you're traveling. Consider the following:

- **Hotels and Motels** including **lobbies, lounges, elevators, pools, coffee shops, restaurants and bars**.

- **Museums, Shops, Restaurants, Parks, Scenic Areas and various Tourist Attractions.**

- **Poshtels** are increasingly popular hostel-hotels where you can stay in a shared or a private room. They are high quality, sometimes luxurious places which offer a common area where guests can go to interact with other international travelers. There may be a bar, a café, and a pool, and there's always free Wi-Fi, a 24/7 reception desk and security. There are many in Europe and a small but increasing number in the U.S. Google "postels" or "hostels" and the name of the city to find them.

- **Commercial Travel Companies Catering to Singles.** A number of companies offer group travel experiences for singles. There are singles tours, singles cruises and singles vacations. If you google "travel for singles," you'll find many possibilities. Some of these travel companies cater to singles in their 20s and 30s, but some also have trips for single travelers over 40 and over 50.

- **Club Med** has several resorts dedicated to single travelers. My girlfriend Elaine vacationed at a Club Med that was not limited to single guests. On her first day, she met a terrific guy, spent her entire Club Med stay with him, and they then had a long distance relationship for a number of months. Neither wanted to move across the country, so the relationship didn't become permanent, but they had an amazing time on their vacation.

- **Singles-Friendly Cruise Lines.** Some cruise lines are especially friendly to single travelers. **Holland America Line** is one of them. The Single Partners Program is offered on most of their cruises and hosts cocktail mixers and games. Holland America also offers a roommate matching service which can save you the singles supplement fee charged on many cruise lines. Singles may dine together by request. Some of the **Norwegian Cruise Lines** ships have a significant number of single cabins and also offer single cruisers a studio lounge with TVs, a bartender and coffeemaking facilities. And there's a daily pre-dinner gathering for single guests. **Royal Carribean** offers a lot of activities for singles and a communal dining table for the sit-down dinner each night. The luxury lines **Silversea** and **Crystal Cruises** are friendly to single cruisers. Other lines can be friendly to singles as well. Be sure to do your research on the particular line and ship before registering for a cruise to be sure you'll feel comfortable cruising alone.

- **Voluntourism.** If you're interested in volunteering on an archeological dig, on an environmental conservation project like coral reef research, teaching English in a different culture, maintaining trails in beautiful spots or working with animals like sea turtles, lions or monkeys, consider a volunteering vacation. Some of these projects are specially arranged for single travelers. Google "volunteer vacations for singles" to learn about the organizations which organize these opportunities. You may very well meet single men who are passionate about the same causes as you. And working with a guy is a great way to get to know him in an unpressured way.

Chapter 38
Tall Men

Many women insist that their Mr. Right be tall. If this is your requirement, you may want to reconsider because you're significantly limiting your pool of eligible good guys.

My old friend Trish, who's about 5'3" tall, had been married to a short guy who became abusive. She finally divorced him after the abuse became physical. Then she dated for years, refusing to go out with anyone under 5'10" because she didn't want to be reminded of her abusive ex, who was short. She did meet several nice guys who met her height requirements — but all of those relationships fizzled out. After 8 or 9 years, she met David, who met all her requirements except that he was 5'8". David fell for her immediately and treasured not only her, but her family. "I can't build you a palace," he said, but I'll always treat you like a queen." Trish decided not to run. She gave herself a chance to get to know David and realized early on that he was a gem. Now, they are seriously considering spending the rest of their lives together.

In addition, some tall women have wonderful marriages to much shorter men. I know two happily married couples like this. One of these couples is in their 40's and the other in their 60's. The wives are at least a head taller than their husbands and this doesn't matter at all to any of them.

However, if you are tall and really want to meet tall men, here are a couple suggestions.

- **Tall People Meetup Groups**. There are meetup groups for tall people in a number of urban areas, including San Diego, Houston, Vancouver, Kansas City, New York City, and Washington DC. Google "tall people meetup groups" and your city to see if there are any in your area.

- **Tall Clubs International.** Tall Clubs International are present in a number of locales. To become a member, women must be 5'10" and men 6'2" tall. They sponsor social events and an annual national convention. Google "Tall Clubs International" to learn more. The club website has information on tall clubs in Europe and throughout the world as well.

Chapter 39
Organize a Monthly Singles Dinner

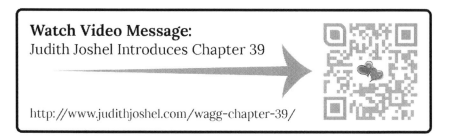

Watch Video Message:
Judith Joshel Introduces Chapter 39

http://www.judithjoshel.com/wagg-chapter-39/

My friend Betty met her husband Rich at a monthly Friday night potluck dinner for single Jews. One Friday each month, people gathered for a potluck Sabbath meal in someone's home. These dinners became so popular that there were too many people to fit into one home. So the potluck dinner was held in several homes and after dinner, everyone gathered in one of the homes for dessert. It was at a dessert gathering that Betty met Rich. This always struck me as a great way to meet guys, and I am recommending it to you. Here's how to get started.

Plan a monthly dinner for singles in your age range. It might be a potluck dinner at your house where everyone brings a dish. It might be a dinner held at a local restaurant which has a room you can reserve for private events. Approach one or two of your single friends and see if they're interested in helping you plan and host it and get the word out, especially to single men who would be interested. Even if none of your single friends are interested, seriously consider organizing this ongoing event yourself.

If you don't want to host the dinner at your home, choose a good local restaurant with a private room as the venue. Choose an evening like Friday or Sunday when people are likely to be available. Then brainstorm on how to get the word out to singles who'd be interested in attending. To start with, you could invite any single guys you know in whom you're not romantically interested and some of your single girlfriends. If it seems there will be more women than men, require each woman to bring a single man who's a platonic friend or acquaintance. This is her ticket for admission.

You'll be feeling your way during the first several dinners. Only a few people may attend at the beginning. Ask each of them to get the word out to others for the next dinner. Attendance should start building. This ongoing event will appeal to singles wanting to meet someone compatible. It's a natural way to mingle with new people and the food will be a draw, especially for single guys who are living on their own and love the chance for a good meal.

Think about how you can spread the word about your ongoing monthly dinners. If you'd like to attract men of your religious faith, post notices in public areas in your church or synagogue and put regular notices about upcoming dinners in the church or synagogue newsletter and website. Spread the word among ministers, priests or rabbis; they often know singles who want to meet someone.

There may be singles meetup groups where you could get permission to make your event one of the sponsored events for the group. You could also create your own meetup group as a way for interested singles to find your ongoing dinner events. There are lots of ways to publicize your monthly dinners. Be creative.

Chapter 40
Your Creative Man Locater Mindset

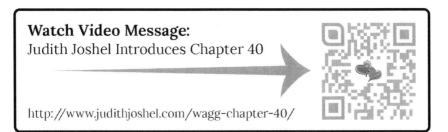

Watch Video Message:
Judith Joshel Introduces Chapter 40

http://www.judithjoshel.com/wagg-chapter-40/

I invite you to try any of my strategies on how and where to meet quality single guys. I also invite you to think outside the box, including my box, and to nurture your own **Creative Man Locater Mindset.** Come up with strategies of your own that feel right to you that could ultimately connect you to the kinds of guys you'd really love to meet.

One way to do this is practice what I call **Thinking Backward.** Here are some examples.

If you want to meet guys who want to be of service, ask yourself where they might be. **Men who want to be of service** may want to know how to help people in emergency situations so you might find some of them **taking or teaching first aid and CPR classes.** They might be doing **disaster relief work with the Red Cross or other organizations.**

A guy who is into technology may be at an Apple Store or a Best Buy or cell phone store or in a computer programming or web design class.

A guy who loves comedy may frequent **Comedy Shows** or be taking a **Comedy Class.**

You get the idea. Figure out what interests your Mr. Right might have and do some creative **Thinking Backwards** to come up with activities and places where he might be. Then take yourself to some of these activities and places and be your warm and friendly self. And if he's not at the first venues you try, have a good time anyway, be creative, and keep trying.

Chapter 41
Miracles Are for You

Watch Video Message:
Judith Joshel Introduces Chapters 41 & 42

http://www.judithjoshel.com/wagg-chapters-41-42/

Do you believe that miracles are for other people — that they will never happen for you? I'm here to say that the miracle of love is for you, that it is your birthright and that no matter what you've suffered in your life, you deserve love. Even if you've been struggling with discouragement and despair for years, you have the power to turn around your luck in love, to find the right guy and to create the loving relationship you desire.

Make a promise to yourself that you will not give up until you've found Mr. Right and created that loving relationship. Use the tips and ideas in this book. I invite you to experiment with them. If something doesn't work, be open to trying it again and to trying new venues and activities.

If you feel driven and desperate to find Mr. Right as fast as possible, and you've been trying for a long time, take a timeout from dating —- a month or two or whatever feels right — and regroup. Put your focus on yourself and your own life and come up with ways to make yourself feel really good. If you feel you need help in this area, consider investing in some coaching. You always have choices. If you are overweight, you can lose weight — or you can own it. Yes, you're likely to attract more guys if you are your optimum weight, but always remember that some men are attracted to curvier women. One of my former clients is what might be considered 50 pounds overweight. Laughingly, she calls herself a big beautiful girl. She wears sexy clothes, has great makeup and hair and is married to a handsome guy who loves her deeply.

Nurture patience and appreciate the life you have. Although you don't have the loving man you want, you can still enjoy and be deeply grateful what you do have in your life. And this attitude is exactly what will attract good men. A healthy guy can tell if you feel good about yourself and your life, and if you do, he's likely to be drawn to you.

During your timeout, use your brilliant brain to map out a savvy man-finding strategy that feels good to you. Use the principles in Chapters 2 through 7 to improve your attitude toward meeting men and dating. Make a list of the strategies in this book for meeting guys that particularly appeal to you. Come up with other strategies of your own. Rank these strategies by priority and when you feel ready to start dating, put one or two into action each week. Sometimes a strategy will work but sometimes it won't. Just roll with it. Either way it's a learning experience.

The key to your success is to stop yourself from diving straight into discouragement, even hopelessness when you try a strategy that hasn't worked. Many women who have found lasting love have been searching for Mr. Right for a long time and have met many Mr. Wrongs along the way. This is surprisingly common. The key for success is not to become discouraged by the Mr. Wrongs. Regard each guy you meet as a chance to practice your dating skills and to get to know someone who may be interesting, even fascinating, even though he may not be right for you.

Above all, keep a sense of humor and lightness about it all. Kathleen and David met online. Their first date was for dinner at a nice restaurant that David had suggested. All went well until the check came. David reached in his pocket to find that in his rush to get to the restaurant on time, he had forgotten his wallet. Kathleen had $11.27 in cash with her and no credit card. David was mortified. He wanted to see Kathleen again and was afraid this would be a deal breaker for her. Embarrassed for David, Kathleen was also amused. She hadn't been wildly attracted to him, but had enjoyed their conversation and was open to seeing him again.

David started calling friends to find one who was free to come to the restaurant with a credit card. The friends he managed to reach were all at a basketball game. One said he'd be happy to come by with his credit card, but he couldn't get there until the game was over in a couple hours. David had no other choice; he would wait. He told Kathleen the plan and said that he'd love to see her again, but he didn't expect her to wait with him. Feeling sorry for him, Kathleen said she'd stay for a little while. Over coffee they started sharing stories of the funniest things that had ever happened to them. They were so engrossed in their conversation they were surprised when David's friend arrived with his credit card. After being "hostage" to an embarrassing experience, Kathleen realized that she had enjoyed David and wanted to get to know him better. That evening was the start of an 18-month courtship. Kathleen and David have been happily married for 6 years, and they sometimes tease each other about whether their romance would have gotten off the ground if David hadn't forgotten his wallet on their first date.

What's the lesson here? I would say it's to expect the unexpected when you're dating, be amused by it, don't let it throw you off center and be open to the unexpected working to your advantage.

I suggest adopting a new perspective. Why not look at each date as a practice run for meeting the right guy? Although your date might not turn out to be Mr. Right, you might find him interesting, even fun. And if you find him dreadful, how about writing the story of this date for a book about your dating experiences which you may or may not publish one day? Writing about your disappointing dates can help you keep your perspective and your sense of humor about the dating process, keep you from despairing, and encourage you to continue until you find your right guy.

Chapter 42
And Finally

If a healthy guy senses that you're needy or even desperate for a man to complete you, he'll usually walk away. If he feels that you're dissatisfied with yourself and your life, he's likely to feel that he wouldn't be able to please you, and he'll probably disappear quickly.

As I noted in Chapter 5, it's important to take a good look at yourself. After you've honestly evaluated your strengths and your weaknesses and made the changes you feel will be helpful — stop judging yourself. Own who you are with pride. Feel good enough about yourself to relax with the men you meet. Stop worrying about their opinion of you and find out who they are. Often just asking the right questions and listening to a man's answers will let him feel that you are a woman to cherish.

I've worked with women who have found Mr. Right within a few months and with others who found him after 2 or 3 years. You can't control exactly when this will happen for you. But you can speed things up by never giving up, being open to trying new things, including things that push you outside your comfort zone, and by reaching out for help when you know you need it. If you are willing to do these things, I believe that you will find love with an amazing guy. I wish you hope and joy on your journey.

If you've been searching for Mr. Right for a while and are having no success, consider getting some help and feedback from a coach or therapist. We all have blind spots, that by definition, we can't see, but often a trained professional will see them clearly. If you want to be notified of group coaching trainings based on this book and other group programs I am offering, or if you are looking for one-on-one coaching, I will be happy to advise you. Here is the link to my contact page: http://www.judithjoshel.com/contact-me/

Above all, be open, warm, welcoming and creative. Remember that your Mr. Right is also looking for you! Use your Man Radar

and your Radically Open Curiosity to help him find you. And remember that you are at your best and most magnetic when you are
doing things you love. Start there with activities and venues you
love and branch out using any of the ideas in this book which appeal to you. Believe in your success and make it your priority to do
whatever you need to do to attract Mr. Right into your life. I am
sending you love and hope.

Appendix 1
Safety Tips for the Savvy Single Woman

Always be mindful of your personal safety. When you're meeting new men, whether on or offline, you want to be warm and welcoming, but you also want to be clear with yourself that you don't know this new guy. There's no getting around the fact that it takes time to get to know someone. Most of the guys you'll be meeting will be good people, but a small number may not be. So you'll want to take some precautions to be sure you stay safe in your early encounters with new guys.

Don't give a guy you've just met a lot of information about yourself. You don't have to tell him where you live or where you work, and you don't have to give him your last name until your intuition gives you a strong message that he's a good guy. Through Google Voice you can get a free phone number in your area code to give to guys you are meeting. When they call the number, the call will be forwarded to any phone number you designate.

You may feel weird not being open about your personal information when you first meet a guy, but you can actually say to him that you don't feel comfortable sharing more personal information right away. It has nothing to do with him, just with your comfort level. A good guy will understand. He knows there may be dangers from people you don't know, and he will want you to feel comfortable and safe. The fact that you take care of yourself in this way tells a healthy man that you truly value yourself.

Get to early dates on your own. Don't let your date pick you up and drive you in his car. And don't let him drive you home until you have a strong sense that he's a good guy. Never go out on a boat with a guy you barely know. A client of mine did that, and I almost had a heart attack. Fortunately, there was no problem, but when you barely know a guy, you want to avoid being alone with him until you know him better and feel good about him. Never go to a guy's home or invite him into your home until you know him reasonably well and feel you can trust him. Going to a guy's home or inviting him to yours is often taken as an invitation for sex. If you're not ready to sleep with him, it would be smart to keep your dates in public arenas. Hikes on early dates are fine if there are other people in the area, but you'll want to avoid hiking into more remote areas.

Tell a friend or relative when and where you're going on early dates, the guy's name, phone number and email address, and anything else you know about him. If you have any uneasiness about him, ask a friend to call you while you're on the date just to check in with you. Although it's usually rude to take phone calls or texts when you're on a date, tell your date at the start that you may be getting a call or text from your friend that you'll need to respond to and apologize for this in advance.

If you're on an early date with a guy you don't know well and need to leave your table to go to the rest room or for any other reason, always ask for a fresh beverage when you return. There are a very small number of guys who may slip a drug into a woman's drink. This happens very rarely, but it did happen to one of my clients. I don't want it to happen to you.

Don't ignore your intuition. If you have a funny feeling about a guy, pay attention to it. Your funny feeling may not have anything to do with him, but then again it may. If your feeling is strong, don't give him personal information about yourself and get away from him calmly, without drama, and as soon as possible.

Don't sleep with a guy you barely know right away, no matter how strong the chemistry. It may not be safe to be alone with him. He may have a sexually transmitted disease he doesn't mention. If he is a good guy and you sleep with him too soon, you can easily destroy the possibility of developing a committed relationship with him.

Stay away from alcohol and weed on early dates. You want to be fully present so that you can evaluate who he is and how he's showing up. Although a drink help you relax and feel less nervous, it may also affect your impulse control and cause you to wind up in bed with your date when that isn't what you wanted to happen.

There's a fine line between healthy concern about your personal safety and paranoia. Choose the healthy concern side of that line; don't let yourself leap into paranoia. Let your mantra be conditionally trust but verify.

Appendix 2
Getting Support on Your Journey
to Mr. Right

I invite you to download your free gifts if you haven't already done so:

Gift #1:

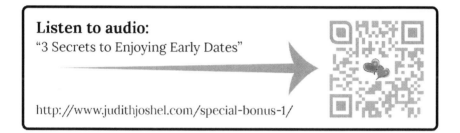

Listen to audio:
"3 Secrets to Enjoying Early Dates"

http://www.judithjoshel.com/special-bonus-1/

Gift #2:

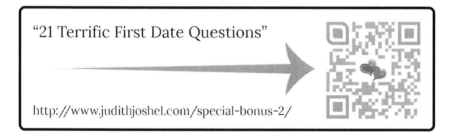

"21 Terrific First Date Questions"

http://www.judithjoshel.com/special-bonus-2/

I am a former divorce attorney mediator and have successfully coached hundreds of women on their journey to Mr. Right. If you would like to explore the possibility of working together, please fill out the contact form at http://www.judithjoshel.com/contact-me/

I work with just a few one-on-one clients and regularly offer Find the Good Guys Group Trainings based on the principles of this book. I also offer longer-term Man Magnet coaching groups to do deeper work on clearing the path to Mr. Right. I invite you to reach out to me.

Made in the USA
San Bernardino, CA
28 December 2019